THE UNIVERSITY OF
WINCHESTER

A Man Without Loyalties

A Penologist's Afterthoughts

Printed by: Biddles Limited, Guildford, Surrey

A Man Without Loyalties

A Penologist's Afterthoughts

A MAN WITHOUT LOYALTIES

A Penologist's Afterthoughts

Nigel Walker

Barry Rose Law Publishers

ISBN 1 902681 40 1

Published by
Barry Rose Law Publishers Limited
Chichester, England

Other books by the same author

A *Short History of Psychotherapy*, 1957, Routledge and Kegan Paul.

The Ascertainment of Mental Defect, 1960, as Chairman of a Scottish Working Party, HMSO.

Morale in the Civil Service: A Study of the Desk Worker, 1961, Edinburgh University Press.

Crime and Punishment in Britain, 1965, Edinburgh University Press.

Crime and Insanity in England, Vol. 1: The Historical Perspective.

Sentencing in a Rational Society, Allen Lane the Penguin Press.

Crimes, Courts and Figures: An Introduction to Criminal Statistics, 1971, Penguin.

Crime and Insanity in England: New Solutions and New Problems, 1973, with Sarah McCabe, Edinburgh University Press.

Behaviour and Misbehaviour: Explanations and Non-Explanations, Blackwell.

Punishment, Danger and Stigma, 1980, Blackwell.

Sentencing Theory, Law and Practice, 1985, Butterworths.

Crime and Criminology: A Critical Introduction, 1987, Oxford University Press.

Public Attitudes to Sentencing, 1988, with Michael Hough, Gower.

Why Punish? 1991, Oxford University Press.

Sentencing Theory, Law and Practice, 1996 edition, with Nicola Padfield, Butterworths.

Aggravation, Mitigation and Mercy in English Criminal Law, 1999, Blackstone Press.

ACKNOWLEDGEMENT

I am very grateful for the help of my daughter, Valerie Walker, who improved my text and has even written a foreword, and of my nephew, Michael Potter, who now and then exorcised my laptop. The staff of the Radzinowicz Library have been as helpful as always.

To my wife of 64 years

CONTENTS

FOREWORD

by Valerie Walker

When I read my father's book, I was fascinated by all the things about him I had not known or had only half known: not because they were secret, but because, I suppose, I was first of all too young to understand, then later not interested; finally, when, as an adult, I would have been interested, I wasn't around to hear about them.

But I was bewildered by two things: first, the title of the book. Certainly, my father is not a man to give his unthinking loyalty to any organization: regiment, civil service, university. But it is clear from what he writes that he worked hard (and, where possible, creatively) for all of these. I think, however, that he saw too clearly the inefficiencies and misguided policies in these institutions to be able to identify himself with them.

In his final job, as professor and departmental head, I know that he addressed himself energetically to the task of raising morale and cohesion: to creating a department to which, if you like, its members could feel loyal. (I find it strange how few heads of departments in university settings and elsewhere see this as an important part of their job; strange because not only do you increase the department's efficiency, but you ensure that you are remembered with affection.) My father made a habit too of being accessible to students as well as staff. He held regular meetings of academic and other staff, which didn't make decisions, but allowed any subject to be discussed. Nor was he inaccessible as a parent, like so many of my patients' fathers.

Nor can I quite accept that his career was a matter of luck. Certainly he had lucky escapes in Canada, Italy and Manchester. But his spare-time PhD and his first books demonstrated his academic inclination. It was his opportunities that were a matter of luck. Nowadays his change of career would not be unusual. Forty years ago it was extraordinary. I can vividly remember the amazement of my friends. My father, I know, was very nervous and afraid he wouldn't be up to it. As it turned out of course he was more than up to it.

Part of the time my work as a clinical psychologist is in what is called 'care of the elderly'. Some psychologists consider that something called 'Life Review' is useful with this age group. Certainly, some patients benefit from help with thinking about their life, especially painful episodes which they have suppressed. Normally life review is something we all begin to do from middle age onwards. But it would be sad if all my father saw was a succession of chance events rather than a well-planned, successful career.

PREFACE

This isn't an autobiography. Few autobiographies are. Only a very abnormal personality wants to put on record its most private pleasures, its worst humiliations or its most discreditable aberrations. But if one has had a life as full of diversions as mine, and with so many slightly ridiculous examples of crucial good luck, there is no harm in trying to share some of the entertainment with a few readers.

The result is best called afterthoughts. This makes no extravagant claim to comprehensiveness or accuracy. One puts down what one remembers, as one remembers it. "My memory is not at all hazy," wrote Evelyn Waugh to Betjeman, "just sharp, detailed and dead wrong". Mine may be less sharp and detailed, sometimes vaguer than I would wish, but never, when I've been able to check it, dead wrong.

Names, however, will be more accurate than dates. There will be plenty of name-dropping, and not much name-suppression. Some of the names will be quite undistinguished, included merely out of friendship, gratitude or vengefulness. Occasionally a name has been omitted for fear of a libel action, or out of compassion. I see no great harm, however, in paying off a few old scores, within limits set by humanity. Revenge is what Bacon called "a kind of wild justice". Anyone who is still alive and regards my justice as too wild is as free to miscall me.

No social historian should make the mistake of regarding me as a typical product of my school, college, regiment, department or academic discipline. It will soon be clear that I have always felt myself slightly alien to whatever subculture tolerated me at the time. I am even disinclined to categorise myself as a criminologist, for reasons which will become clear later. I have been a man without loyalties. Friendships and enmities are more rewarding.

1. DAMNED IN THE CRADLE

"Porridge tomorrow? Yes, if we're spared"
(Nurse Cook)

How should mere memoirs begin? Not with 40 pages of genealogy, like Anthony Powell's autobiography. His father was 'affronted' by genealogies, and scared of what his own might disclose, but his son managed to claim a tenuous connection with that tedious hero Marmion. I took no interest in my forebears until after my eightieth birthday, when a letter arrived from a Walker in Australia. He had hired a genealogist in Edinburgh, who traced his lineage back to a mid-nineteenth-century ancestor in Fife. That Walker had emigrated to the Antipodes in the late eighteen-fifties. His brother had stayed in Fife, becoming a station-master only to be run over by a premature express train. This confirmed his relationship to me, since there was an oral tradition in my family that exactly this fate had befallen my great-great-grandfather in Oakley. I was more interested in the fate of the émigré, and hoped at first that he might have been a transported felon; but by the date of his voyage Australia had ceased to assist the motherland in this way, and was even asking Britain - tongue in cheek - to take some Australian felons. My great-great-uncle's voyage was almost certainly voluntary. His descendant told me nothing about himself or his branch of the clan, and our correspondence petered out in spite of my efforts.

My own father, Edinburgh-born, was the British Vice-Consul in Tientsin, having started his career in Canton. After learning Cantonese - a difficult dialect - he then had to learn Mandarin when transferred to Peking, and became famously fluent in both dialects. My mother had become engaged to him in Edinburgh, but it was three years before she was allowed to join him, travelling economically across Europe and Asia by the Trans-Siberian Railway, escorted only by a missionary's wife, and hoping that she wouldn't regret her promise. Two of their three children were born in Tientsin.

Unless one is a novelist or a sociologist it is probably a handicap to be born in an unheard of mining town. It certainly is if the mining town is in North China. People back in Britain had heard of Peking, but not of Tientsin. In fact it was no mean city: a flourishing but untidy conglomerate of European buildings, surrounded by a plain of loess, a muddy river and the shacks of poverty-ridden peasants. It stood on a navigable river, and British troops had used it as a base for the march on Peking at the time of the Boxer rebellion. By the end of the First World War it was divided into 'extraterritorial concessions', administered and policed by Britain, America, France and Russia. The German concession had been taken over by Britain, and our family moved into it, attracted by a spacious stone-built house with airy verandahs.

Only a short walk from 13 Yunan Road was the river, broad and turbid, where sampans dodged about between barges and steamboats. Most of the sampans belonged to fishermen and their cormorants. These unlucky birds dived all day for fish they couldn't swallow because their throats were ringed. Just before dusk the rings would be removed to let them feed themselves. This was one of our spectator sports.

The summers were sunny enough to give me skin cancer in later life, in spite of our solar topees, and hot enough to drive us to the seaside for a couple of months. Bei-ta-Ho, later a favourite resort of Mao's elite, was just a boring beach to us; but Wei-Hai-Wei had junks, sampans and hillsides with mulberry bushes, where we collected silkworm cocoons to hatch back at home. Wei-Hai island was a naval base with a vivid and snobbish social life, but the mainland harbour was small, used only by the occasional junk or sampan, and ideal for swimming and diving. One of my early visual memories is of another small boy bobbing upside down, rather like a fisherman's float, because his lifebelt had been strapped on below his centre of gravity. As I watched, his legs waved more and more feebly, until our Nurse Cook jumped in fully clothed and saved his life.

Sharks were almost unheard of here, but typhoons were a threat, throwing junks about and confining us to the solidly built hotel, where at six I received a proposal of marriage from a spotty playmate called Doris, confirming Nurse Cook's belief that children mature too early in tropical climates. Even better than Wei-Hai was Ch'in-huang-tao, where the seashore pools were full of tiny swordfish who pricked one's fingers with their tiny charges, and the marsh inland was alive with bullfrogs and brightly coloured but harmless snakes. The bullfrogs' tadpoles were large and green, and the bungalow had plenty of huge terracotta barrels where they and the snakes could be lovingly reared. Further up the coast was the end of the Great Wall, visible but not visitable because of the fear of bandits.

Fears of this and other kinds limited us quite a lot. Warlords' armies fought bloody battles outside Tientsin, and their wounded were brought to the city's hospitals. Even in peaceful times the countryside was thought to be too full of bandits for safe excursions, although in his younger days my father had travelled to the edge of the Mongolian desert, where he was briefly imprisoned on suspicion of being a spy - a suspicion naturally encouraged by his consular passport.

Disease was another fear, especially of my mother's. Milk and water had to be boiled, and fruit soaked in Jeyes Fluid. The calendar was filled with vaccinations, inoculations, wormings and circumcisions. Certainly smallpox, dysentery and meningitis were almost endemic amongst the poor Chinese whose shacks were so close; and of course our Chinese servants were regarded as potential carriers. Minor infections were undeniably common. A grazed leg or arm would suppurate for weeks. European children did die of sudden fevers, and I remember worrying my parents by insisting on being taken to see the grave of a schoolfellow I had hardly known. We went on a beautiful evening, with high cirrus clouds reflecting the sunset. Even now, 80 years later, that sort of sky is a *memento mori* for me.

Fears of death were encouraged by Nurse Cook. At first my sister and I were looked after by Amah, who like all our servants was a relative of our Number One Boy, Yang Tai. Amah was tirelessly kind, and incurably superstitious. Babies' navels could be penetrated by evil spirits, but penetration could be prevented by a barrier of silver. So a silver dollar would be surreptitiously slipped under the sticking plaster over the umbilicus, to be removed by my mother but to reappear next day, until a word was had with Yang Tai.

Sadly, Amah was replaced, first by the flighty but friendly Nurse Shaw (one for the soldiers, it was said) but then by the austere Nurse Cook. Having been a teacher in Aberdeenshire she was really a governess, but Nurse Cook was what she was called till the end of our lives. She came to Tientsin by way of northern India, and her tales of tiger shoots made her popular with everyone but me. For me she had a grimmer side. She was a Calvinist, and I was one of the damned. She had access not only to this information but also to some source of pamphlets which sought to instil the fear of God by means of stories in which children died, slowly and full of grace. In one story three children lived in houses whose gardens backed onto three sides of a graveyard, and soul by soul and piously they each went under the sod. Death was never far from Nurse Cook's mind. If we asked whether we could have porridge next day her invariable answer was 'if we're spared'. It was her equivalent of 'Insh Allah', but less optimistic.

Her mind was not only godly but dirty as well. In the summer, when we slept on the verandah, my sister and I would sometimes get into the same bed and tell each other stories - until Nurse Cook found us. There was hell to pay, but it was a hell without an explanation. Even our parents, who were conventional but tolerant, seemed unable to tell us why what we had done was not done. From that time on, however, I was the object of Nurse Cook's unremitting suspicion, especially when six-year-old Doris proposed marriage to me in the hotel corridor. She prowled the bedrooms at night, and even after she left us I had nightmares in which a hand would reach under the bedclothes and seize mine.

The anthropologist Ruth Benedict used to distinguish societies in which guilt was all-important from those in which shame took guilt's place. Pre-Maoist China was a shame society. Avoiding loss of face was more important than avoiding sin. Even my parents worried about what friends might be saying about our move into the German Concession, or my father's decision to leave the consular service for a business post. When Yang Tai reproved us children it was for endangering 'face'. He and Nurse Cook, though in no way inspiring, gave our inwits two kinds of agenbite.

At the same time Nurse Cook was a good teacher, better than some of the staff of Tientsin Grammar School, as we were to find. The school was in the British concession, but took children from all the nationalities in the city, except of course Chinese. And of course it taught Latin and French, but of course not Chinese. Like children in British India we were to be shipped back to a country which would have no use for eastern tongues. The irony was even sharper because our father was a superb linguist, who had been given prizes for his Cantonese and his Mandarin, and was chosen to act as ADC to the last Emperor, Pu Yi, when he fled to Tientsin. He brought Pu Yi to our school, and we bowed to him. But my father was a very busy man, and so was Yang Tai. What we learned of the language was imparted by our rickshaw coolie - another relative of Yang Tai's - who taught us what to shout back when Chinese children taunted us on our way to school. He did not tell us what the phonemes meant, but they were offensive enough to provoke showers of stones, and obscene enough to get him into real trouble with Yang Tai. Apparently most of them involved accusations of incest. He was rather too small for the rickshaw, and by jumping up and down in the seat we could lift him an inch or so off the road. When we could afford a car he was promoted to chauffeur and the rickshaw disappeared. Car journeys were safer from stoning, but less fun.

Our father resigned from the Chinese Consular Service, in which promotion meant waiting for dead men's desks, and accepted a job with a wool exporting firm, whose success was guaranteed by the peculiarity of North Chinese sheep. Their wool was so tough and wiry that it doubled the life of carpets, and was much in demand in Europe and the USA. The wool was bought from Chinese 'compradors', a Portuguese title which may have originated in Macao. They were the only Chinese whom we entertained socially - apart from Pu Yi, of course - and that only once a year. The gulf between the British and the 'natives' was even wider than in British India. Only the missionaries really bridged it, and only they had the hardihood to live outside the towns. The missionary children, unlike our schoolfellows, spoke real Chinese. The Dunlop twins even spoke it to each other, which made them unpopular.

Golf was our father's favourite game, and he was North China's Champion for several years. Later he beat me 6 and 4 at Mortonhall on his 70th birthday. The Tientsin golf course included land that had been a Chinese burial ground, with tumuli whose tops could be flattened to serve as tees. Even at the age of five I felt that this showed a lack of respect for the dead; but perhaps my preoccupation with my own after-life made me oversensitive.

Suddenly all this came to an end. The Japanese prepared to invade Manchukuo, and my father foresaw at least some of the horrors that were on their way. He got all of us except himself a passage on SS *Patroclus* from Shanghai. I can still recall waving tearfully to him through the fog at Taku Bar as our steamboat left for Shanghai. He stayed behind only long enough to transfer his business to northern India, and from then on we saw him only when he could afford a holiday - about once every three years. At least his foresight spared him the fate of friends who were interned by the Japanese. Conditions in their village were nowhere near as bad as in prisoner-of-war camps; but food and medicines were scarce, and some friends died, including Eric Liddell, the Olympic quarter-miler. Our closest friends, the Stirlings, had moved to Shanghai, where they felt safer; but when they did leave it was in the middle of a Japanese air-raid.

We had sailed home once before, via Yokohama and the Canadian Pacific Railway. But this would have meant time spent in Japan, and we took the long route via the Suez Canal. Our mother had just had a baby, and six weeks with three children in hot cabins taxed her strength and temper. Fortunately the strong and saintly Nurse Cook was still with us. My recollections are of watching flying fish and porpoises in blinding sunlight; of days ashore at Singapore, Penang and Colombo; of being taught to box on a blistering foredeck in the Red Sea; of watching Stromboli's glow at night, accompanied by a well-informed lecture on volcanology from Nurse Cook; of my sister's vomiting for a day and a night in the Bay of Biscay.

2. On Not Skipping Backwards

"But passing such digressions o'er ..."

(Walter Scott)

Edinburgh seemed a cold, unwelcoming city. It was our parents' home town, and we had been there once before. All I recall of that visit was being gassed on my grandmother's ironing board to have my tonsils cut out: a botched operation that had to be repeated six years later. There were plenty of uncles, aunts and cousins because my mother had been a seventh child, but we seemed more than a little outlandish to them. My mother was always afraid that her older siblings would disapprove of our behaviour, or standard of living, or choice of schools, or our father's absence. Scotland is both a guilt culture and a shame culture. (England is a shame culture, Ireland a guilt culture, Wales a culture of cunning, as I was to discover years later in the army.)

It was 1927, the year of the total eclipse of the sun. For me and my sisters this was no big deal. Darkness, in our experience, was an everyday occurrence. All I recall are the coloured strips of celluloid we were given, which were fun to peer through anyway. The same seems to be true of other people who were children at the time, although BBC interviewers seem to have found octogenarians who are prepared to recall feelings of awe. There was certainly less media-generated hysteria than in 1999.

It was several years before we saw our father again. He had managed to set up his wool exporting business in north-west India, where the wool of the hill sheep was as wiry and valuable as in North China; but it was a long time before he could afford to visit us. Throughout our teens he was with us for only a month or two every three years. His business nearly failed during the depression of the early thirties, but eventually recovered and expanded. Our

8

mother talked frequently of rejoining him in India, but somehow we knew she wouldn't. In a way we were a one-parent family, yet did not feel like one. So far as I can tell our parents were faithful sexually and emotionally. His life had as its centre the Karachi golf-club, and I think hers was made tolerable by family, friends and bridge. When our father did come home he must have found it hard to adjust himself to a noisy family with unfamiliar interests.

He seemed immune to the diseases of the East. One morning in Karachi he found his manservant in bed with a high fever, which his doctor diagnosed as bubonic plague. The bungalow was quickly surrounded by a *cordon sanitaire*, until a more experienced doctor arrived. "You are very lucky, Mr Walker. This is merely a very virulent kind of smallpox." The servant survived and my father didn't contract it, but smallpox was suspected when soon after his arrival in Edinburgh one summer he developed pustules and a high fever, and had to be segregated in a bedroom. It turned out to be merely a spectacular chicken-pox. I used to suspect that he went back to India with relief. We did not really get to know him until he retired after World War II.

Meanwhile we moved from rented house to rented house - 13 in 10 years - because of our mother's fantasy of going to live in India. When she was feeling well-off the houses were roomy, stone-built houses in 'the South Side', and we had a maid, a dog and a garden. When she wasn't we had a flat and a 'daily'. Sometimes in August and September we simply gave up an Edinburgh home and moved to Elie on the Firth of Forth. My father felt especially at home there, as his father and forebears were Fifers. Elie was becoming a popular holiday village for golfers, and we certainly played a lot of golf. But one round is very much like another, and what I recall with more pleasure is the exploration of the coast, and especially its cliffs and rock pools. Neap tides were times of particular excitement, when we could reach pools that held small octopi, lobsters or partan crabs. Forrester, the golf professional, who knew my father well, would take me out shooting - below high-watermark of course, where nobody's permission was needed.

I was also taken shooting when I stayed with my uncle at his farm in Suffolk. He was a rather dour man, but I was fond of the woman he lived with, and when her divorce eventually allowed her to marry him we called her Aunt Phemie. She was especially kind to me when I was afflicted with severe insect bites, and would administer her own special lotion in the middle of the night. I was distressed when she was later named in the local press as the chief suspect in a murder case. A neighbouring farmer died of a poison which had been mixed into his Kruschen Salts, probably on the evening of a bridge party attended by my uncle and Aunt Phemie. She certainly had a violent temper, was known to have quarrelled with the farmer, and during the bridge party had used his bathroom where the Kruschen Salts were kept. It was one of those cases in which nobody is charged in the end, and the suspect is never exonerated. I couldn't help thinking that Aunt Phemie was probably guilty, at least of manslaughter, but I continue to cherish her memory.

When I was a year or two older I bought my own .410 shotgun - no police permission was required in those days. My father, who arrived home from India at the time, was worried sick, but instead of using his *patria potestas* he quietly convinced me that I wasn't yet a safe owner of a hair-triggered firearm. I was grateful to him for not simply ordering me to take it back to the shop, which I nevertheless did, getting my money back from a slightly guilty shopkeeper. It may have been my father's reasoned handling of family problems which made me so unprepared later, in the army and the civil service, to accept unexplained orders or decisions by senior officers or politicians. More simply, it may have been his absence for so much of the time that made me intolerant of authority - of ministers of the church, housemasters, platoon sergeants, company commanders, staff colonels, committee chairmen, politicians, college heads.

In Edinburgh I felt a failure. I had been a successful Wolf Cub in Tientsin, but in the Palmerston Place Scout Troop it was found that I couldn't skip backward: I still can't. I was thus ineligible for any badges. I was a day-boy at the Academy, at first in Miss Fuller's class. For some reason the fact that I'd been brought up abroad, and didn't have a recognisable accent, irritated her. Accents were very important in Edinburgh, and accepted as indicators of social class. A BBC accent ranked high: a glottal stop very low (it's interesting that the glottal stop has now climbed up the ladder, and can be heard at Eton and Cheltenham. I know of only one other European language in which it is fashionable - Danish).

At the age of nine I wasn't percipient enough to see that Miss Fuller was deliberately making me feel stupid. It was a feeling that I have never quite lost. Anyone who contradicts me confidently can make me unsure. Fortunately when I graduated from Miss Fuller's class to the Upper School I was under first-class teachers, but for several years I was convinced that the bottom of the class was my proper place. My mother had anxious talks with the Rector, P.H.B. Lyon, whose metier was charming parents but who cut no ice with boys or masters, and certainly not with me.

It took Latin and puberty to rescue me. We had got past Caesar, and the decent obscurity of a foreign language allowed us to be introduced to poetry, romantic and scurrilous - Horace and Catullus, Martial and eventually Juvenal. Billy Peel and 'Cod' Rowe were superb classics teachers. Rowe was also a ferocious user of the tawse, a three-inch wide leather strap. This could do great damage if applied to the buttocks, as it once was by an ignorant new master from England who wouldn't listen to the advice of his class and nearly flayed off a boy's trousers. Applied to the hand it was agonising but not disabling, and Rowe was very accurate. It was odd that he should also be a good teacher. He taught me to write Latin verse, and one holiday I translated *Sohrab and Rustum* into Virgilian hexameters. We were introduced to Greek rather late, and I never found it as congenial.

Our introduction to English literature was less professional. I know of only one English scholar produced by the school in my generation - J.I.M. Stewart, whose conscientious book about Kipling was insultingly ignored by Angus Wilson's. His novels are better known. They are sentimental about the Academy, and about Christ Church, where I later met him briefly. His donnish allusions to the better-known poets and painters allow the reader to feel cultured as well as entertained. His 'whodunits' - for which he used Michael Innes as a pen-name - are deservedly famous: *Hamlet Revenge, Murder at the President's Lodgings, Lament for a Makar*, and many more. His hero was unusual in the detective genre: a middle-ranking policeman (later promoted to an unlikely eminence) who was neither aristocratic nor alcoholic, happily married and faithful to a woman of good family who had never been raped, kidnapped or addicted. One could read the books at the end of a trying day without being shocked or too engrossed to put them down. Unlike today's *romans policiers* they are untainted by the dirty realities of crime, procedure or forensic evidence, and when I met Stewart in his sixties I was able to confirm that he wasn't interested in them. His Oxford novels are another matter; but of them more later.

The Academy's science teachers occasionally produced outstanding men. James Clerk Maxwell belonged of course to a past generation; but Kenneth Craik was a pupil in the nineteen-twenties, and made his name in artificial intelligence at Cambridge before being killed in a bicycle accident in 1941. One of our stimulating science teachers was Wightman, who was also a philosopher and historian of science, and wrote a book about monism. He managed to interest me in the philosophy of science, a subject I chose many years later for my doctoral thesis.

School life in those days was less exciting than it must be now. Illicit drugs and teenage pregnancies were unheard of. Smoking was heavily punished, and bullying was rare because the prefects - preciously called Ephors - regarded it as their prerogative. They, unlike the masters, were allowed to beat our buttocks, but only with a clacken, an enormous wooden spatula with which the younger boys played a hockey-like game in the septic gravel of the school yard. In China I had acquired some degree of immunity to infections of scraped skin, but the aboriginal children of Edinburgh festered.

After school, cricket or rugby were compulsory - not soccer, which was for state schools, like marbles. Cricket could be avoided after a certain age by rifle-shooting at Dreghorn in the Pentland hills, where I witnessed enough accidents - luckily non-fatal - to make me see my father's point. Rugby could be avoided by boxing, as the reek of male sweat still reminds me. It was only in the boxing ring that I discovered how much shorter my arms are than average. This was no handicap at chess, but that was played surreptitiously in the library, and none of the masters took an interest in it.

Then my mother decided that, having only sisters and an intermittent father, I needed to be toughened by becoming a boarder. The two years that followed were the worst in my life. Even as a recruit in the Royal Scots Fusiliers I never saw bullying of the nastiness I witnessed and occasionally experienced at Scott House. The other Houses may have been better run, for all I know. Scott House was run by a married master who lived in separate quarters. An unmarried junior master and a matron lived in our half of the huge building, but seldom entered the dormitories. The real managers were three brothers, sons of a Highland farmer. The eldest was officially head of the house, and made the rules. His brothers were his enforcers. Rugby and cricket was their world, and on Friday nights the younger boys had to know the names of the school team for next day by heart or be beaten with gym-shoes. They were not really given to bullying themselves, but tolerated it. Whether they knew that older boys were taking younger ones into their beds in other dormitories I am not sure. I didn't at the time associate what was happening with sex. I don't think force was ever used. The younger boys simply liked having a protector. It was probably true of most boarding schools. As for the bullies I have often wondered whether they were simply typical of the rough Highland or Border farms from which they came, or were envious of boys from different backgrounds. Day boys regarded the Houses as a tribe apart, and preferred not to associate with them, but my friends treated me as an exception because I had been 'one of them'.

The friend I saw most of was Bill Calder, one of three brothers who, like me, had been brought to Edinburgh from a foreign school. In their case it was the Schloss at Salem in Germany. Their father, Sir William Calder the epigraphist, had been an admirer of Salem's headmaster, Kurt Hahn, and probably helped him when, as an émigré, he founded Gordonstoun. Bill told me that it was his father, too, who, as an undergraduate forced to pass a Divinity exam, had spotted that Christ must have been born a few years BC - one more reason for ridiculing the millennial celebrations. The Schloss school had made the Calder brothers rather Teutonic, but as day boys the worst they had to put up with was being laughed at. It was Bill with whom I walked in the morning across the meadows to catch the tram to school, and who introduced me to the pleasures of hill-walking in the Cairngorms; but when he took me hunting for capercailzie with a shotgun I found I had lost my taste for killing birds.

On Sundays at Scott House we put on starched collars and kilts, even if our parents were Lowlanders, English or Boers. Since one of my grandmothers was a Ross I did not feel quite so phony as some, and I got used to the kilt later in the army. As everyone knows, it is a sawn-off descendant of the Highlanders' great-cloak; but not everyone knows - or admits - that the innovation was the work of a Lancashire mill-owner, for the convenience of his Scottish workers. As a garment it is pretentious without any special utility, and it has its drawbacks. In winter the hem gets wet and even icy, chafing the legs. It is supported only by its tightness, and middle-aged wearers develop distinctively displaced pot-bellies. The jacket has to be of a special short cut, so as to allow for the exuberance of the sporran (but full-bearded sporrans are properly worn only by the military). Even without the theatrical trappings such as the *skean dhu* it is hideously expensive, but lasts a lifetime, sometimes two. A grandson-in-law wears mine.

Most of the tartans were invented about the time of Sir Walter Scott, who made other contributions to his country's narcissistic myths. His *Rob Roy* (the Scottish equivalent of Robin Hood) was the subject of a repertory company play which toured the country in those days, and was as popular as the pantomime. It was a vehicle for the chauvinism which has since developed into separatism. The climactic scene shows Rob Roy, captured by the redcoats, standing on a bridge with his elbows tied round a musket. He holds this position while the drumbeat swells, and then does what the yelling audience knows he will - snaps the musket with one tremendous convulsion of his pectorals and escapes in an unexplained blackout. I believed that the war had put an end to this folk-play, though not to the state of mind; but in 1962 a naive nationalist revived the play for the visit of King Olaf of Norway, to the embarrassment of right-thinking Scots.

Walter Scott can hardly be blamed for the play, but his novels, which were obligatory reading, could be culpably tedious and lacked any humour. Strangely, Prince Albert thought them too 'demoralising' for his sons. As for Scott's epic poem, *Marmion*, it takes over a hundred stanzas to get our hero from Whitby to Edinburgh, name-dropping all the way:

> But, passing such digressions o'er,
> suffice it that the route was laid
> across the fursy hills of Braid.
> They passed the glen and scanty rill,
> and climbed the opposing bank until
> they gained the top of Blackford Hill.

What makes this comic, I think, is not simply the guide-book bathos. Tetrameters are for pantomimes. *Hiawatha's* trochees are as comic as *Marmion's* iambi.

Terms in the Houses were nasty, brutish and far too long. We juniors had to get up early to fill the cold baths and empty them after everyone had dipped. Dressing, breakfast and a mile-and-a-half dash to school encouraged constipation. The school lavatories were fouler than any I saw in the Army. School lunches were better than Scott House's meals because the masters had to share them - a device which I later tried to introduce into the country's 'approved schools'. Back at Scott House too little time was allowed for supervised homework, so that I had to finish mine in the lavatory after lights out, sitting on the wooden O in the small hours of midwinter translating Georgian poetry into Ovidian pentameters. This was regarded as eccentric by the Highland brothers but for some reason not punishable.

Eventually my parents realised that if I was to fulfil their scholastic ambitions - which were high - I would have to become a day boy again. From that time on school was enjoyable. I captained the small-bore rifle team that won the national shield, and got into the Bisley shooting eight, along with my other close friend, Jock Rushforth, later a Commando Major. My boxing was less successful because of my short reach - a handicap in rock-climbing too, as I found later.

Edinburgh Academy prided itself on getting Oxbridge scholarships, and most of my classical friends went to Oxford. I stayed at Christ Church for the examination, and met the awesomely erudite products of Eton, Winchester, Shrewsbury and St Paul's for the first time. By the hour of interrogation by five dons I was in despair, but managed to contradict the classical scholar Denis Page about Virgil, which must have won me a vote or two. Christ Church offered me an exhibition. My reaction was to hope for a scholarship at a smaller college, but back in Edinburgh, Lionel Smith said 'Take it'.

Lionel Smith had succeeded P.H.B. Lyon as Rector, and had strengthened the Academy's classical teaching. He was respected because he had been a friend of Lawrence of Arabia, and educational adviser to Faisal. Soon after becoming our Rector he had been offered the headship of one of England's most prestigious schools, but had felt in honour bound to stay at the Academy. This made him popular. Less popular were his invitations to spend a few days at his Bamburgh home in midwinter, because of his liking for swimming in the North sea - for example across to Holy Island. I had the courage to stay ashore, and he had the decency never to remind me of it.

Later, when I was an undergraduate, he used to ask me to take Latin classes in order to allow a master to take the rifle team to Bisley. The boys knew that I was still a teenager, not a real master, and set out to make me lose my temper. I did, and slapped the ring-leader hard on the side of his head. There was a shocked silence, followed by an embarrassed cease-fire. I had shown that I too could break the rules. I expected to be asked to explain myself to Lionel Smith, but wasn't. Perhaps the boy told his parents, perhaps not. Perhaps they thought little enough of it. Those were the days of the tawse and the clacken. With corporal punishments of this kind in daily use it is perhaps not surprising that a slap on the ear caused no scandal.

That was my last contact with the Academy for the rest of the century. In 1999 the school decided to publish a sort of D.N.B. of alumni who had distinguished themselves, in one case by committing murder. Most of them, of course, were safely dead. Exactly what had distinguished me I was not told, but was instructed to write what was, in effect, my own obituary. This seemed to me only fair. Posthumous obituaries not merely deny the pleasure of reading them to those who would most enjoy them, but also deprive them of the right of reply to any unfair comments or omissions. Yet to write one's own was an unusual and humbling assignment, which made me realise just how much I have owed to luck, sometimes quite spectacular, at various junctures of my career.

3. CITY OF EXPIRING DREAMS

"Why do you say 'irron' instead of 'ion'?"
(A socialite from Lady Margaret Hall)

I went straight from a middle-class Scottish school to an aristocratic English college. In those days 'gap years' were an almost unheard-of luxury. My first term at the House - as I learned to call Christ Church when talking to fellow-inmates - was not happy. My school-friends were at other colleges, making new friends. New acquaintances - even other freshmen - were immensely intelligent and sophisticated. My accent was uncouth: I said 'irron' instead of 'ion', as a girl kindly pointed out at a party. My rooms were in the notorious Old Library, where the Steward put newcomers whose financial resources were uncertain. They were certainly low-rented, but also ill-lit, reputedly haunted, dirty, and three floors and a quad away from sanitation. My scout made me nervous. Unlike novelists' scouts he was neither domineering nor servile - just suspicious. I contracted the Old Library Cough, which lasted most of the term, and was probably a defeated attack of tuberculosis (to which the man below me certainly succumbed).

Lionel Smith, Oxford-bred of a formidable mother known as the Tigress of Balliol, cannot have realised that the House was not the most congenial of colleges for a Scottish Academy boy. It is true that I came up at the same time as a Fettesian - Donald Morrison - and another undergraduate from the Scottish industrial belt; but we were amongst Etonians, Wykehamists, Salopians, Rugbeians and Westminster scholars. The landed gentry were also over-represented, as sociologists would say. Their social focus was the Bullingdon Club and its point-to-points. The drunken blasts of its hunting-horns - no horns of Elf-land these - were allowed to terrorise the college every Friday evening. Hilaire Belloc was right when he wrote that members of the upper class adore the sound of breaking glass. For more detail see *Decline and Fall*, and of course *Brideshead Revisited*. Evelyn Waugh was not at the House, but had more friends there than at his own college.

Talking of breaking glass reminds me of King George VI's coronation, in my second year. Everyone dining in Hall was allowed, after drinking the new King's health, to throw his wine-glass into the fireplace, so that it could never be used for another toast. Four hundred not very expensive glasses were smashed that night, in the House alone. Some of us finished the evening by punting up the Cherwell with a litter-basket full of fire-lighters flaming on the bow. When we passed Magdalen Wilfred Kup demonstrated his head for heights by walking up - and more hair-raisingly down - the steeply sloping pediment of the New Building.

Older and more staid were the Rhodes Scholars, such as Arnold Smith, the future Secretary of the Commonwealth. They were really postgraduates, mature, experienced and career-minded; but since they were reading for the same degrees they treated us as equals, and helped us to grow up.

The Students - as Christ Church's fellows were called - did a great deal for freshmen by way of hospitality; and indeed my first human contact with the House was the kindly but egregious Dundas. He visited my mother and me at home a month or so before I was due to come up. More than once as an undergraduate I spent weekends at Laurel Hill near Stirling, where he lived with his sister during vacations. Here again one was expected to bathe before breakfast in icy water, this time the Teith, a small and far from clean tributary of the Forth. My second morning's dive left me with a superficial wound on the chest from some sunken farming equipment. I was introduced to other features of English life, such as *The Times'* crossword - and dinner-jackets. The Dundases' genealogy was impressive, and included Baron Dundas, who in the nineteenth century was known as the uncrowned king of Scotland. Cockburn's memoirs unforgettably describe the Town Council of Edinburgh as 'omnipotent, corrupt, impenetrable, existing only to do the will of Dundas'. The Dundases were landed gentry, and dressed for dinner - but only in dinner-jackets. When I later read E.M. Forster's *Maurice*, in which the three undergraduates at a country house decide to wear dinner-jackets instead of tails that evening because nobody else would be there, I could not believe that he knew what he was talking about; but perhaps he did.

J.I.M. Stewart portrays Dundas as Lempriere in his four-volume novel about the House, but also, much less charitably, in a short story. Nor does the published memoir of him do him complete justice, because it ignores the rumours instead of refuting them. What made D. the subject of gossip was his interest in sex. Every one of his young male guests - none were women - were sooner or later invited to his study to make sure how much they knew about it. He did in fact fill several gaps in my knowledge, and if his interest was prurient - as I later realised - it was not obtrusively so. Once at a lunch party he asked a Rhodes Scholar 'Are you hairy like that all over ?' It was behaviour like this that made him, like Miss Brodie's pupil Rose Stanley, 'famous for sex'; but rumours that he tried to do more than talk about it were to my certain knowledge unfounded. Years later, when he was in his seventies and had become a friend and occasional dinner-guest at my college, he became unexpectedly self-revealing, and told me of two sad aspects of his life. He had spent 30 years compiling a heavily annotated edition of Thucydides, only to have the almost complete manuscript stolen, with his luggage, on a war-time train journey. I have heard this story treated with scepticism because he published so little, but I found it entirely credible. It has to be remembered that in those days handwritten scripts were common, especially when Greek texts were the subject, and photocopying was in its infancy.

The other thing he told me was sadder still. He had always felt exclusively homosexual, but had been restrained by rigid moral scruples. There were of course dons who were known to seduce or be seduced by undergraduates, but D. was not one of them, although as a younger man he had had to bear the burden of listening to Auden's boasts of successful seductions. If I am breaching a confidence it is to kill an unfair rumour, and repay some of his kindnesses. For example, being tutor in Greek history, he would even contribute out of his own pocket to help pupils visit Greece, something I could not have afforded, and probably wouldn't have considered if I could. With D.'s help Donald Morrison and I did the Grand Tour of the Aegean as third class passengers (in bunks in the cargo-hold) of the *Laetitia*. In the museum at Athens I bought a postcard of the statue of a local deity, partly because I liked the look of him, partly because he was said to bring luck. It seems an appropriate frontispiece.

Other tutors were Barrington-Ward, Denis Page, later Gilbert Ryle and Michael Foster. Denis Page was one of the classical scholars who believed that the somewhat different vocabularies of the *Iliad* and the *Odyssey* was evidence that they were composed by different people; but of that more later. He also found credible evidence, later discredited, that the plague of Athens was measles.

At this time, in my first term, he made me feel that as a writer of Latin I had a lot to be modest about. He was particularly critical of my Latin verses, and it would not have occurred to me to compete for the Chancellor's Prize for an original Latin poem if the subject for that year hadn't chanced to suit me. It was Delphi, and I was feeling very disenchanted with religion at the time. Not only was I still resenting - as I have all my life - Nurse Cook's assumption that I was one of the damned ; but I had been on fond terms with an Anglo-Catholic girl in Lady Margaret Hall who had just decided to become a nun (in the event she didn't, but I wasn't to know that). I let off steam in a short Latin poem, in the style of a eclogue, about the futile destiny of the Delphic priestess, and submitted it without telling Denis Page or anyone else.

Expected to get the Prize was Trevor-Roper, who had been runner-up before. He probably would have got it this time - his poem was certainly longer - but Fraenkel, the refugee professor from Germany, held out for my poem on the ground that it had more feeling for the language. This was one of the many occasions in which luck has given me a helping hand. Page and Barrington-Ward were embarrassed that they had not known I was a candidate, and Barrington-Ward merely pointed out my single mistake (the gender of laurels). I had three rewards, however. My father had just come back from India for a holiday and was able to be in Oxford to hear me read the ritual extract from my poem at the Encaenia. The College made me an Honorary Scholar, giving me the right to wear the long gown - but no more money. And the University published the poem, so that when I acquired an academic c.v. my bibliography began in my eighteenth year. Back at Edinburgh Academy Cod Rowe could deservedly boast that in the same year two of his ex-pupils had taken the prizes for both Latin and Greek verse, the latter going to my friend Hector Thompson at Magdalen.

All this may give the impression that I was a model undergraduate. On the contrary. I got my First in Honour Mods, the literary first half of Greats, but after that it was downhill all the way. Or most of it. Everyone relaxes in the summer after Honour Mods, but I went on relaxing. Greek history bored me, for Dundas, however kind, was uninspiring. So was Lewis on Roman history, which in those days ended, believe it or not, in AD 63. I had wanted to change my subject to psychology, but was told that this was only for postgraduates. In my day Oxford's only psychologist was William Brown, the Reader in Mental Philosophy, forbidden by the statutes to engage in experiments. (A generation later psychology was an option for undergraduates, and my daughter exercised the option.)

So I had to soldier on at Greats, the most pretentious form of illiteracy on offer at Oxbridge. Fortunately I enjoyed the philosophy, which was not confined to classical authors. But it stopped when it had reached a really interesting stage. Wittgenstein was not recognised by the examiners, and we read the *Tractatus* furtively in punts. My philosophy tutors were Michael Foster and Gilbert Ryle. Ryle, who looked a little like Muggeridge, became famous later for *The Concept of Mind*, translated into umpteen languages. Once in Milan I came across a book called *Lo Spirito come Comportamento*, a much better title which sums up the book in four words. He was an exacting tutor. I needed that, and responded, so that by the time of Finals he was talking about a possible research fellowship; but my history let me down. He was not popular amongst pupils, but when he became Editor of *Mind* he treated contributors as if they were undergraduates, reaching over their dead bodies to rewrite whole paragraphs. As editor he was in a strong position, but this was an abuse of it. He was amusing, but not kind. When I failed to get the expected First he sent me a far from consoling note, saying that he knew I would as soon as he heard I'd become engaged.

Michael Foster, my other philosophy tutor, did not achieve the same degree of fame. He was a reserved and depressive man who looked like James Mason in his film role as Rommel. Unexpectedly he accepted our invitations to join us in reading parties, notably one in the Cairngorms, where he turned out as strong a hill-walker as Bill Calder. Sadly he became more and more depressed, lonely and ascetic during the war years, refusing to eat at High Table because its meals were better than undergraduates. His depression did not end when the war was over, and one night after dining in Hall he put his head in his gas-oven, leaving only an apologetic note for his scout.

Ayer I would like to have had as a tutor, but he preferred candidates for Modern Greats (Philosophy, Politics and Economics: 'PPE'). He had just published his iconoclastic *Language, Truth and Logic* , which demolished metaphysics, so that he was the thinking man's Guevara. He had not by then acquired a reputation for womanising, and seemed to spend most of his spare time wandering round Peckwater Quad, deep in what looked like - and to be fair probably was - logical positivist thought, twirling his well-known watch-chain round his index finger.

Another conspicuous but unapproachable figure was old S.G. Owen, who came in to dine dressed in a dinner-jacket and gum-boots. He lived on Boar's Hill, famous for mud, and saw no harm in scattering it over the Senior Common Room. Years earlier he had published - I think in the *Classical Quarterly* - an article on Juvenal. Housman in Cambridge regarded Juvenal as his preserve, and attacked the article so viciously that Owen published nothing more until Housman died, many years later.

Among my innocent pleasures were the debates of the Twenty Club. Membership was the result of invitations, limited to House undergraduates, although dons such as Gilbert Ryle were often guests. A biographer says that it was elitist after the war, but in the thirties no elite, whether social or intellectual, could be said to have included me. Its debates were not as high-minded as the Cambridge Apostles, but part of the entertainment was the difficulty of remembering to observe its intentionally elaborate rules.

Discipline was exercised by the Senior and Junior Censors. In the days of my delinquencies the Junior Censor was Michael Foster, who never let friendship interfere with just deserts. It was like being court-martialled by James Mason, playing Rommel. I had no dealings with the Senior Censor, Bobby Longden, a much more flamboyant figure, who dealt - not very firmly - with the Bullingdon Club's excesses, and gave tutorials with nothing but a towel over his knees. He became the Headmaster of Wellington and was killed at his front door by a stray bomb in 1940.

My delinquencies were not very exciting, and I can recall only one that was out of the ordinary. A man from Corpus and I were dining with a girl from L.M.H. on the first floor of a restaurant called L'Etoile D'Or, which had indeed a large golden star hanging outside. I think she was the girl who asked me why I said 'irron' instead of 'ion'. The great golden star was within reach through the window, so we unhooked it and smuggled it out under a raincoat. It looked well on a punt, but the girl from L.M.H. didn't want much more to do with it, and the time came when it was necessary to get it back from the upper Cherwell to Christ Church. The raincoat covered it, but we made the mistake of detouring through back streets, and were stopped by an unnecessarily alert policeman, who asked us what was under the coat. I can still remember the unveiling of the giant star, like Perseus displaying Medusa's head to his pursuers. The policeman, however, was not petrified, and marched us to his station. As undergraduates we would normally have been bailed at once to our colleges, but my friend gave his name as Denzil Dunnett, which it was, and was thought to be taking the mickey. We spent an hour or two in the cells (which were later refurbished as the St Aldate's public lavatory) until the sergeant was persuaded to confirm from Corpus that they had a man of Denzil's name. We were not guilty of theft since we had not intended to deprive L'Etoile permanently; and in fact they got the star back before they had noticed its absence. We were simply fined by the Proctors.

Discipline was not really intrusive enough to halt the dissipation of my second summer and autumn. For one thing I had slightly more money to spare than I need have. My sources were my college exhibition, a scholarship from school, and £100 a year which my father insisted on scraping together even in the years of the depression. It might have been better for me if he hadn't. I got drunk a little too often, saw too many films and spent too much time on the river. Punts and Wittgenstein were not the river's only attractions. Punting a canoe was a trick which seemed worth learning at the time. In a canoe one could enter the underground Trill Mill Stream and be carried, in what looked like a sewer, under Carfax and Christ Church. For claustrophobes the relief was almost spiritual when they emerged into the Isis below Folly Bridge. I'm told that this particular pleasure is now impossible.

Hospitality was another trap. The day might begin with a guest for breakfast, although often the guests were uninvited. The worst of them were from the Oxford Group, notably an Edinburgh Academical called MacNicol, who saw me not as damned but as ripe for salvation. It took a lot of invective to rid me of this turbulent pest. Less easy to get rid of, because he was a family friend whom my mother had asked to keep an eye on me, was the slightly older John Summers, who later became a missionary in Rhodesia. To do him justice he was simply keeping his promise to my mother, not trying to save my soul but merely pointing out how I was wasting the best years of my life. He was right, of course: I was behaving as if there were no tomorrow. As it turned out, for some of us there wasn't, but 1938 was too early for that sort of excuse.

A few of us saw the war as inevitable. One was Philip Hunt, whose family spent most of their holidays in Bavaria or Austria. Another was Wilfred Kup, who was to be killed as a fighter-pilot. Most of us, however, had our heads deep in the sand. We weren't sympathetic with German aspirations, like some of the Cliveden set. We simply didn't want the warning signs to be real. Life was too enjoyable. A few Jewish refugees were arriving, and we knew that many Jews had lost property and jobs; but at that time there was hardly any news of atrocities. What we did know was that while Germany had been rearming this country had not, and that an armed confrontation would cost us many lives. There were silly stories that the German tanks in the photographs were made of plywood, but they were not believed. We did not know quite how out-of-date our own military equipment - and military leaders - were, but we knew that we were no longer a military nation.

As for the Scots, we felt at one remove. Douglas Young, the nationalist, even challenged Chamberlain's right to declare war on Scotland's behalf, and was treated as a conscientious objector. A Scottish university demonstrated its patriotism by sacking him. Douglas Young had endeared himself to me long before I met him by a short article in a literary journal. Denis Page and other scholars were arguing that the same man did not write both the *Iliad* and the *Odyssey* because the vocabularies of the two epics differed, sometimes using a different word for the same thing. Douglas Young's article showed that by the same token Milton could not have written both *Paradise Lost* and *Comus*.

The summer of 1939 brought retribution for wasted terms and vacations. In the winter and spring I had tried to make up for them, but managed only a Second. The gruelling Greats exams were followed a week or two later by the long-drawn-out Home Civil exams, for which I had entered when I realised that my chances of an academic career were dwindling. Donald Morrison, with whom I shared lodgings, had done the same, not being academically inclined, and got both a First and the top place in the Home Civil list. Fortunately the philosophy examiners liked my papers, and their enthusiasm got me a high enough place to let me choose my department. By that time war was upon us, but at least I had a job.

4. A RELUCTANT WARRIOR

"Officers of field rank may add, if they so wish,
'God Bless Him'"

(Mess rule)

I chose the Department of Health for Scotland because I thought its concerns were important - I didn't discover how boring until later - and preferred to work in Scotland, where my fiancee was a medical student. We were very conscious that it was only a matter of a month or two before I would be called up, and in December we ventured on a marriage that has lasted 64 years.

My first job as an Assistant Principal was the vetting of designs for centres for decontaminating victims of gas attacks. I recall one plan which would have obliged naked women to scurry down the same corridor as naked males. Handing over my first job, when I was called up, was a transaction which made me feel slightly bitter, because my replacement was of the same age. No doubt I was being irrational: he must have had some disability, but etiquette was more delicate than in 1916, and nobody to my knowledge asked him why he was 'reserved'. My friend Bill Calder was also reserved, but everyone realised how bad his eyesight was.

My introduction to the army that January was the racecourse at Ayr, which had been turned into the training centre for the Royal Scots Fusiliers, a regiment I had nothing against but had never heard of. Hardened recruits slept, in January, in the windswept grandstand. New arrivals were allotted in threes to loose-boxes which were comparatively sheltered but smelt of horse as well as feet. I shared mine with a tax-inspector and a miner, neither of whose names I can remember now. I was lucky not to be in the same loose-boxes as some of the Glasgow recruits, whose hair and feet smelt worse, and whose language and topics of conversation were fouler than anything I had come across before, even at Scott House.

The tax-inspector was uninteresting, but the miner and I had at least one thing in common: a liking for hard-boiled eggs (of which more in a later chapter). Many of the badly nourished Glaswegians had never even seen one. They left them uneaten, so that the miner and I had most of them. He was a prodigious eater, indeed a semi-professional one. He went in for pie-eating contests in Gorebridge, and won one on a week-end leave. Sadly, his opponents had dropped out so soon that he had spent most of his prize-money on fish and chips. He was courting a girl back at home, but could not read or write, so that we had to play a major part in his correspondence with her. It occurred to us - or to me at any rate - that we could have had some fun with it; but his physique was so massive that it would have been foolhardy. We got him engaged, but were parted before he got married, which I hoped he would because he was so likeable.

The first few weeks were very like the OTC camp-life at school, with the difference that this was winter and the NCOs were real. They had more in common with the Glaswegians than with us easterners, but weren't brutal or unfair. After six weeks I graduated to the chilly grandstand, but my school OTC certificate soon whisked me off to the Officer Training Unit at Dunbar. This was a relief. It wasn't that life at Ayr was unpleasant: it was more easy-going than I had expected. It wasn't that I saw myself as a leader of men: I never did and never was. But it looked like postponing for a few months the dreaded arrival at the front in France. A front there still was that winter, before the German attack through the Low Countries.

Dunbar was far more demanding than Ayr. NCOs called you 'Sir', but only as a preliminary to some humiliation. At dawn we prepared for room inspections, with particular attention to the correct folding of blankets, but not overlooking the need to Brasso the metal of the light-bulbs. Breakfast was eaten at full speed, lest there be no time to empty the bowels. Later there would be drill by sergeants from the Guards, weapon training (including 'the naming of parts' made famous in the poem), and in the evening the study of King's Regulations. In full marching order we crawled in mud, swam in the icy harbour, panted up and down the Lammermuir hills. Disciplinary penalties consisted mostly of unpleasant chores, but looming behind them was the threat of RTU - return to unit. In 1940 the course was six months long, and several of us did not make it. One committed suicide with his rifle one night; but it was rumoured that he had more serious worries as well.

A vivid memory from Dunbar is of a boxing tournament in which everyone had to fight. I was drawn against a man with arms as long as an orang-utan's, who had been a public school champion in his teens. I had boxed halfheartedly at school, and lasted the fight without being knocked out, but vomited all night - a sure sign of concussion. Nevertheless I managed to parade next morning, and was comforted by hearing that Hutton had reported sick with a broken thumb.

More historic is the memory of the Great Stand-to, when the rumour that Hitler's operation Sea Lion had been launched sent nearly every soldier in the country to man the beaches. We spent the night digging slit-trenches in the Berwickshire dunes and peering anxiously out to sea. It was my first experience of the loosening of the bowels which comes with the prospect of being attacked. I found - and others told me the same - that it is only the situation of being a sitting target of an intentional attack which has this effect. Other kinds of danger don't. One of my fellow cadets drank a half-bottle of whisky on an abnormally empty stomach, and was duly RTUed next morning (he was *very* drunk). By dawn the alarm had been diagnosed as false, and we marched back to work.

Drunkenness was the cause of many a Return To Unit. Another cadet in our cohort destroyed his military career on the eve of being commissioned. The military police found him drunk in the High Street with a paper bag in his hand, singing 'chips today, pips tomorrow'. For him there was no tomorrow. The sin seemed venial and the penalty excessive.

By that time we had been asked what regiment we wanted to be posted to. I knew nothing about any regiments, and I had no qualifications, such as a modern language, for any special unit; but my mother had talked about a distant cousin in the Cameron Highlanders, who sounded a romantic body of men. So I put them down.

The 5th Camerons were not romantic. They were a territorial battalion of Invernesians which had been sent to Thurso, the northernmost town on the mainland, presumably to repel landings in Caithness and Sutherland. After a fortnight's leave in Edinburgh, where I had to spend a lot of my pay on officer's kit, I arrived in the September dusk at the camp gates, a year after the declaration of war. Caithness consists of a treeless plain of mud plastered on an impervious layer of stone which makes excellent paving but prevents water from percolating. The camp therefore floated on two feet of mud. Mud was everywhere. The Nissen huts were joined by duck-boards, but it was easy to put a foot wrong in the dark. Gum boots could be worn off duty, but were often sucked off and engulfed, like the horse in *Black Beauty*.

The officer detailed to greet and steer me in the dusk to my hut through the mud was a territorial called Bobby Sims, a young English manager from the Kinlochleven aluminium works. This was the beginning of a friendship which probably saved my life in a roundabout way, and which lasted until, long after the war, he was sent by British Aluminium to Sydney, where he died. He saved me many a time from ridicule - for example when I tried to bring an

English officer's cane on parade, instead of the Highland regiments' ash-plant. He made peace between me and my company commander, a handsome regular officer called Noble. Noble caught me explaining to my platoon why they had just been ordered to hand in their brand new socks and draw still newer ones. I forget why, but apparently it was not good for discipline to explain reasons for orders.

The other new officer from Dunbar, Colin Hamp, fitted in more easily. He did not suffer from my tendency to resent being ordered about, and made a point of getting on well with his company commander. I think I was the only officer with a degree, and the fact that it was an Oxford one, not a Scots one, made it worse. I was not the only new officer to be regarded as *outré* however. A young Argentinian, called Cabrera, had been so proud of his Scots ancestry that he had enlisted voluntarily and asked for a highland regiment. Neither his English nor his deportment were of a high standard, but he did not deserve to be treated with ridicule. We were like a class of 15-year-olds which must have its target, and he was it. I think he was eventually posted away to some other unit. So was the black Invernesian private whom General Wimberley noticed in the front rank of A Company just before we were sent to guard Balmoral. Today he would have been inconspicuous. He did not get to Balmoral.

Guarding the royal family at Balmoral for a month or so in summer was serious business, done with live ammunition 'up the spout', patrolling the grounds all night. Whether the German High Command ever contemplated an attack here I don't know. I came into no contact with any member of the royal family, but caused the princesses to giggle in Crathie Church when I fell asleep in my pew after a night on patrol. The penalty for amusing royalty was an extra tour of duty as 'orderly officer', whose job it was to inspect almost everything two or three times a day. My second tour of duty at Balmoral was more eventful, but that was in a later incarnation.

The penalty was awarded by the adjutant, Maitland-Makgill-Crichton, who particularly disliked me. He was a career officer, only a few years older. With his thin and sandy hair, pale face and thin mouth he was the *doppelgänger* of the modern actor Nicholas Jones. It was of course the duty of an adjutant to make life hell for second lieutenants, but Sandhurst had equipped his natural sadism with special military skills. His office sergeant, with whom he had a close relationship, acted as his informant, and could be relied upon to bring him the gossip from the sergeant's mess about junior officers. That winter the General Staff had decided that the new army's weakness was the quality of its junior officers. Like Nurse Cook's belief in predestined damnation it was the explanation of everything that went wrong, especially on tactical exercises. If senior officers were ever to blame we never heard of it. When one became a major one was of 'field rank', which seemed to guarantee quality, and allowed one to wear a smart fawn overcoat called a 'British Warm'. One Seaforth Mess even had instructions for toasting the King on Mess Nights which ended "... officers of field rank may add, if they so wish, 'God bless him'." Captains and lieutenants might not.

Many years later Alanbrooke's *War Diaries* for 1942 gave me a glimpse of another perspective. "It is all desperately depressing ... Half our Corps and Divisional commanders are totally unfit for their appointments, and yet if I were to sack them I could find no better ..." In fact he records so many sackings for which he was responsible that one wonders what happened to his victims. I wonder whether a contempt for one's subordinates was endemic in the regular army.

The Camerons' Mess Nights were almost as ritual as the Seaforths', and Maitland-Makgill-Crichton thought that they would be improved if officers bought 'blues and trews' to wear at them, instead of khaki and kilts. This was at a time when the army was retreating in North Africa, the Merchant Navy was losing ships in the Atlantic, and England's cities were being pounded by the Luftwaffe. The adjutant did not dare make his inspiration an order. We were simply told that the Commanding Officer hoped that we would comply (I doubt whether he really cared). Infantry officers - like their men - were the worst-paid in the services. We officers had had to buy our uniforms, and the hope that we would buy blues as well was resented. Some of us temporary gentlemen did, but most didn't, and the Adjutant realised that he could do nothing about it.

Another romantic idea of his was that men should wear their kilts 'in the field', as they did in the 1914-18 war. Now the kilt is a handsome garment for a parade or a dance, but in bad weather it gets as sodden as blotting-paper; and when it freezes the icy fringe saws at the legs. It is impossible to vault barbed wire without entangling the kilt. Only in fording rivers does it have an advantage over trousers, and that is only because it can be taken off without removing boots. Adjutants are sheltered from these harsh facts, but he was eventually convinced.

A stronger CO would probably have kept him in order. Our Colonel Cattanach was a territorial, an architect by profession, and was in awe of regular officers from Sandhurst. About this time I was relieved of my platoon and made Intelligence Officer, which brought me into more contact with him. I had to learn to ride a motor-cycle in order to follow his car, which was driven at high speeds. On icy highland roads I came near death oftener than I did in Italy. When maps had to be read I rode in front, and could keep our speed down, but at the risk of going under his wheels. Like most territorial COs he was replaced before the battalion went overseas, and I am glad to say that he survived the war. He was a likeable man, and I had nothing against him but his failure to keep his adjutant in order.

One of my friends in the battalion was Pipe-Major Ross, who was not only a superb piper but also an architect in civil life. When not required to pipe he was the Warrant Officer in my Intelligence Section, and suggested that we could produce large-scale maps in quantity for battle exercises by a simple piece of equipment which used daylight printing paper, and so needed only sunlight. He and I would draw the maps for exercises, and by evening every officer had a copy. This was an immediate success, eventually copied by some other battalions, but only, I think, in the 51st Division. Poor Pipie survived the North African desert campaign, but died after the war of emphysema, possibly the result of piping through the Libyan sand. A regiment's pipers were so important to its morale, especially on long marches, that they were seldom used in battle, but acted as stretcher-bearers - not as safe as it sounds.

Step by step the battalion was moved south, and it became disquietingly likely that we would soon be sent to the Middle East. By the time we were stationed in Aberdeen Bobby Sims had been posted to Dunbar OTC as an instructor, although he rejoined the battalion in time to be wounded at Caen. Hayton Camp was in a part of Aberdeen where the local inhabitants disliked any soldier - even or perhaps especially a Gordon - and no doubt our Invernesians' off-duty behaviour was equally aggressive. However that may be, so many bricks were hurled over our barrack fence at night that we had to wear steel helmets when within range of the perimeter. The rest of Aberdeen was hospitable. By that time officers were allowed to live in digs with their wives, and most married subalterns did. Most of the Invernesians and regulars, however, were not joined by wives, and found temporary consolation in the city, as I learned from overheard conversations in the Mess. A curious feature of this extra-marital activity was a tendency to hunt for one-night stands not singly but with one's closest friend, possibly so that one could compare notes next day, as I heard some of them doing. Oxford had taught me that it was not done to name the lady; but this convention did not seem to be recognised in the Camerons.

That and whisky-drinking were the Invernesians' evening activities. To have 'drink taken' was an excuse that had to be accepted for most misbehaviour in the Mess. Once an officer left the Mess he had to look sober, and everyone managed it. Not all the other ranks did. The Provost Marshall and his men patrolled the streets each evening on the look-out for misbehaving Jocks. I recall one disciplinary hearing when the Provost Marshall testified that he had seen the accused weaving about in the street. "I approached him and told him to take his hands out of his pockets. He told me to go and fuck myself. I acted accordingly - Sir!"

Buchan - the country north of Aberdeen - is not highland but rural in a way of its own. Horses, in the shape of the garron, were still important to its farming, and garrons are almost intractable. So it was essential for a ploughman to learn 'the horseman's word' - a secret, magical word that would make the beast obey. Young ploughmen were taken at dead of night to remote bothies, blindfolded and asked if they dared take 'a shak o' Auld Horny' (i.e. shake the Devil by the hand). If they dared - and some didn't - the cold foot of a dead calf would be put in their hand, and they would be told the Horseman's Word. There were still old men in Buchan after the war who remembered the ordeal but wouldn't reveal the Word. I once told a Hungarian professor this, and she said that there were still Magyar peasants in her country who believed in the secret Word, although perhaps not the same Word.

While I was soldiering in Buchan, mapping fortified beaches and such-like, I heard from my mother that Nurse Cook was alive but not well in Huntly. In fact she was bed-ridden with arthritis, but well looked after (I think with help from my father). She was touched to be visited, even by one of the damned. I felt priggishly charitable, but at the same time strangely moved to see her again. She died later in the war.

Bobby Sims probably saved my life at this point. He made a good impression on the CO at Dunbar (General Alexander's brother) and when asked if he could recommend anyone else from his regiment offered my name. I had managed to scrape an A grade as a cadet - probably by surviving the boxing match - and the posting came through quickly. What astonished me about the choice of officers as instructors for Dunbar was that, three years after the start of the war, so few of us had taken part in real fighting, whether before Dunkirk or in the Mediterranean. We were very conscious that some of our cadets had experienced battle, for example at Dieppe.

I found myself appointed Weapon Training Officer, and after an intensive course set about making sure that every cadet had actually used every infantry weapon, from the Mills grenade to the 3-inch mortar, not on parade grounds but on moors and in woods. Standing by cadets who were nervous about throwing their first live grenade, and occasionally dropped it, was a jumpy morning's work, even when we had solid cover to dive behind. Grenades were the usual cause of fatalities in training, but after my 18 months at Dunbar I could boast that no cadet had become a casualty of my realistic training.

I was less lucky with my unfortunate sergeant, Calderwood. It was our job to deal with every unexploded grenade, shell or mortar bomb in the Lammermuirs area, where the Polish Army left plenty. When the grenade was a plastic one it was usual to dispense with the gun-cotton primer, detonator and fuse recommended in the text-book, and simply fire a rifle at it from behind cover. When I was doing this one day I told Sergeant Calderwood to take cover as usual, and after giving him enough time to do so exploded the grenade. Unfortunately he had stood up to watch, and a fragment blinded him in one eye. There was an official court of inquiry, at which he himself acknowledged that he had not obeyed my order, and held me blameless. My defence was that I was entitled to assume that he had obeyed it - an unusual reversal of the defence of acting under superior orders. Against me was only the fact that my technique was not the one in the book. I was officially censured. Poor Calderwood was apologetic.

The Lammermuirs were 'fair polluted', as Calderwood put it, with unexploded 25-pounder shells left by the less scrupulous Polish gunners, and for shells we had to use the full detonation kit. Shepherds had been warned to leave them untouched, but one shepherd's son found one of these large yellow objects above his cottage, and rolled it down to show his mother. She admonished him severely, and put it on the mantelshelf. The shepherd said he'd take it down to the police next time he went to Dunbar. She wrapped it up, with a string handle, and he took it on the bumpy bus journey down to Dunbar, accompanied by his collie. At Dunbar he dumped it on the desk of a horrified inspector at the police station. From then on it was handled with orthodox delicacy, and exploded - behind sandbags - with unimpaired violence. The Angel of the Lammermuirs had been on duty that week-end.

Another job was organising an opposed landing at night under live Bren-gun and mortar fire at Belhaven beach. With parachute flares, buried explosives and tracer bullets visibly close overhead, we put on, every six weeks, a show on which I was congratulated, even by the cadet who had been at the Dieppe landing. Unfortunately on the first night I had omitted to warn Scottish Command, with the result that the Navy at Rosyth put several armed craft to sea to deal with the invasion. Another reprimand, but this time no casualties. The only fatality in thousands of hours of realistic weapon training occurred, by sheer chance, a day or two after I left. A cadet mishandled a rifle-propelled anti-tank grenade. The supervising sergeant, lying beside him, should have noticed but didn't, and was killed. It was ironical as well as tragic, because this weapon was obsolescent by that time.

5. LUCK IN ACTION

"There are no atheists in foxholes"
(Anonymous)

But that, as I say, was after I left. My time at Dunbar was the most enjoyable part of the war. Our daughter was born during it. So was the Sims' daughter. My wife's readiness to move home to be near me whenever this was allowed had been good for my morale. The other officers - even the Guards adjutant - were congenial, efficient and considerate. I felt that I was doing a job quite well. And the enemy was still at a comfortable distance. The time for a posting came all too soon. Coldwell, the CO whose kindly effectiveness had raised Dunbar's already quite exacting standards, took care to find a decent posting for every departing instructor. Bobby Sims, who felt at home in the 5th Camerons, went back to them (and was wounded at Caen). I had no such feeling for the Camerons, and Coldwell, who knew of my addiction to hills, had me posted to the Lovat Scouts.

This, the most highland of regiments, had been formed by Lord Lovat in the Boer War, to fight on horses, although it had often been dismounted and used for sniping and reconnaissance. Many of its men were ghillies or crofters, and made excellent snipers and observers. Its record in the Boer War and on the Western Front in 1916 and 1917 had made it famous. In 1940, however, after abortive plans to use it in Finland and Norway it had been sent to guard the Faroe Islands - a task which involved more hardships and dangers than one might have expected. Coldwell's grapevine had told him that they were to be trained and equipped as special mountain troops. They were sometimes mistaken for a commando because Shimi Lovat was a well-known officer in the Commandos; but he had left the Scouts early in the war.

By the time I joined them the Scouts were in Thurso, and returning to the Caithness mud made me feel like a loser on the Snakes and Ladders board. Things were different, however. The camp was no longer on the mud above Scrabster but in the grounds of the castle. Kilts were not part of the uniform, because riding garrons in kilts is uncomfortable. My Cameron ash-plant was replaced by the highland *cromag* , an etiolated crook whose extra four inches make all the difference on the hill. Officers carried the stalking telescope, an expensive and bulky instrument, but more powerful than binoculars. Most of the men were still crofters and ghillies from the north-west and the Hebrides, but with the addition of townsmen from the Scottish cities, a mixture which sometimes boiled over. Unlike other foot-soldiers we never - at least in my Hebridean squadron - sang on the march, perhaps because most of our marching was over heather. Perhaps this is why there are no Gaelic marching-songs. But on the road we usually had the pleasure of a piper, and our pipers were famous.

We were organised by territory in an almost feudal way. B Squadron (i.e. B Company), in which I found myself, came from the outer isles, and its Squadron-Leader was Simon Campbell-Orde, whose family had been landowners there. Although he must have been in his forties he managed to stay with his squadron throughout the war. My own 'troop' (i.e. platoon) came from the two most peat-bogged islands, North Uist and Benbecula. Their language was Gaelic, and although their English was passable I could hear the corporals translating my orders to their sections, with an occasional English word such as 'foresight' or 'magazine'. Naming of parts was done in English. I was again made weapon training officer, but it took me some time to discover that naming of parts in the Scouts had not yet told them some crucial facts: for instance that the seven-second Mills grenade fuse had been replaced by a four-and-a-half-second one, and I wasn't sure that I managed to impress everyone with the importance of the difference. One of the men in my troop was of such low intelligence that his corporal warned me never to let him handle a grenade, and we never did.

When it came to rifles, however, the men were experts. Most of them poached deer when at home, and were natural snipers. They were good, too, at living off the land, chiefly with a fish-hook, and they could carry heavy loads up and, more important, down hill. This was vital, because a landing in Norway was planned as part of the Second Front. Or so the Germans were meant to believe. I learned the truth later from Sir Michael Howard, the military historian, and it was worthy of Gilbert and Sullivan. Only Churchill himself hankered for another landing in Norway, having a penchant for Dardanellish enterprises. His Chiefs of Staff were horrified, and every few months had to talk him out of the idea (see Alanbrooke's *War Diaries*). They even offered the task to the Canadians, while privately warning them that it was considered 'impracticable'. In the end we were lucky to be made part of an enormous bluff. As for the enemy, it was only Hitler who was seriously worried about a possible landing in Norway. His generals were not, or they would have added to their 12 divisions there, the minimum considered necessary for internal security.

Whether effective or not, the bluff was carried to elaborate lengths. Norwegian interpreters were recruited, maps and guidebooks assembled, snowshoes were ordered, antifreeze was stockpiled. Four divisions were stationed in Scotland. The 52nd Highland Division were being trained as mountain troops in the Cairngorms, and the Lovat Scouts were to be trained and equipped elsewhere to operate under more severe conditions and further from sources of supply. We were to have no heavy weapons - only rifles, tommy-guns and grenades. Even the Brens weren't really light enough, although we had them officially. We were to learn rock-climbing and skiing - but not, thank God, seamanship. Norwegian officers were attached to us.

Simon Campbell-Orde himself was the most likeable senior officer I ever served under. Almost middle-aged, clumsy, wearing his bonnet at a civilian angle, he was uncannily like his caricature in Leslie Melville's history of the Scouts. Unlike Noble in the 5th Camerons he never gave a tiresome order without an explanation. His reproofs were mild, but remained in one's memory like a burr in one's kilt. His sense of humour was a relief when things went inexplicably wrong. He was shy, however, and a little cut off from his mainland colleagues. This may be why B Squadron always seemed to be isolated from the rest of the regiment .

Just before rock-climbing began we were suddenly told that we were to form the Balmoral guard for that summer of 1942. We felt competent at the operational task, but were modest about smartness. We had a lot to be modest about, as the saying goes. Some uniforms were in good repair, some not. Some men had puttees, some gaiters. Some tried to get away with shaving every second day (they said that they had joined the Lovat Scouts instead of the Camerons because they had been promised that this would do). As for the officers, even the King commented that their uniforms seemed to vary. "It is a tradition, your Majesty," explained Simon "that no two officers should be dressed alike." This tradition was reinforced when half a dozen officers such as I had been seconded from other regiments. There was no question of our being required to wear the regimental riding breeches. I, for example, was allowed to keep my Cameron kilt, but wore the Scouts' blue bonnet. Otherwise only our pipers wore kilts. Fortunately none of the royal establishment tried to inspect us, although the Queen occasionally embarrassed the men by strolling into their camp in the woods to chat with them. I, on the other hand, had a chance to inspect the revolver carried by the middle-aged police inspector who was the King's personal bodyguard. The barrel was rusty, and even the ammunition looked old. In the Army he would have been 'on a charge'. He had never had occasion to fire it, even on a practice range.

The junior officers whose job it was to lead the nightly patrols round the castle were billeted in a cottage in the garden, but their other job - after a few hours sleep - was to play games with the teenaged princesses on the lawn. 'Grandmother's Steps' and 'Stone Tig' were the favourites that summer. Margaret was knocked down during Stone Tig, and slightly injured. In the 5th Camerons the guilty subaltern would have paid the price with an extra night patrol; but our adjutant was fairer. A more welcome perquisite of the guard was a day's stalking. In the Camerons I had poached hinds in Glen Affric in the winter to eke out my company's rations, but this time was lent a Mannlicher and led up Glen Callater by a stalker. I was afraid of merely wounding the beast, which would have meant a real loss of face, but fortunately made a clean kill of the stag chosen by the stalker - a 'puir back-going beast'. Its horns adorned our hen-house in Edinburgh for some years.

Some officers were invited to dine with the royal family, more or less at random. Simon and I were chosen one night. When we entered the drawing-room the King was waving a Garand rifle which he'd just been given on a visit to some American Army unit. He put it to his shoulder and aimed it here and there. At one point I was looking down the barrel and he was fingering the trigger. There was no way of knowing whether anyone had checked that it was unloaded. Ducking was possible but treasonable. Eventually the long moment passed. Later I wondered how my death would have been hushed up. My wife knew where I was; but what would they have told her? Would I have been buried in Crathie graveyard or deep in the forest of Lochnagar?

It was startling to see how much make-up the King used. Few

people realised how far from well he was - and how shy. Luckily it was Simon who was seated beside him at dinner, while I was between the Queen, who did her best to put me at my ease, and Princess Elizabeth who - at 16 or 17 - was almost as tongue-tied as I was. 'Grandmother's Steps' and 'Stone Tig' did not seem suitable subjects for the dinner-table. The King joked about an earlier evening when dinner had been enlivened by a burst of submachine-gun fire just outside the window, and I had to admit that one of my corporals had stumbled while carrying a Sten-gun. A Sten-gun was a tricky weapon, cheap to manufacture but liable to go off if the butt was dropped too heavily on the ground. If we had been equipped with tommy-guns - as we were in Italy - there would have been no accidental burst. By the grace of God no bullets went through the dining-room window.

Some of our own ghillies were not above poaching deer on the royal estate, and not before time we were off to Snowdonia for the rock-climbing. In those days climbing boots had tricouni nails, and several thousand nails scratching at the novices' routes on Faith, Hope and Charity above Llyn Ogwen produced such a high polish on the holds as to raise their standard of difficulty by at least one notch. Some of our instructors were well-known experts. Mine, Wigram, had been a member of a prewar expedition to Everest. Unlike one or two of my men I was not a natural rock-climber, but he forced me to lead to the limit of my ability, having indeed to rescue me on one route with a hastily contrived 'top rope'. Sadly he fell to his death on the same face after the war. Mackenzie and Hargreaves were two other instructors, and Smythe joined us in the Rockies. In fact they trained us to manage climbs of a difficulty much greater than we were ever likely to face in action. More useful was being taught how to manage heavy loads (including stretchers) on moderately steep rocks.

My job as weapon training officer brought me clashes with

Welsh sheep farmers. I set up a range in a valley behind the Carnedds, and allegedly caused most of the local ewes to lamb prematurely. The army paid the first of the many claims, but the numbers became quite implausible, unless sheep were being deliberately driven there in the hope that they would abort. There was also a rather implausible accusation of rape against one of our islanders, who was acquitted. I had to defend a man at a court-martial in a pathetic case. Like me he was not a real Scout, but a regular who had been posted to us after years in the Middle East. Suddenly he was told that he was to be posted abroad again. Brooding, he refused to go on parade next morning, and was court-martialled accordingly. I tried to get the court to empathise with his state of mind, but did not save him from a long period of detention - which ironically postponed his posting abroad.

Next we were shipped to Canada for snow and ice work. Not in a convoy but in a liner fast enough to be risked on its own, the *Mauretania*. As a troopship it was far from ideal. The officers and warrant officers were reasonably quartered three or four to a cabin, but the other ranks slept in hammocks below the waterline. My orders, if the ship was to be attacked, were to join them with my revolver loaded and shoot if there were a dangerous rush for the companion-ways. In fact I spent most of the voyage suffering from influenza and sea-sickness. We sailed into New York one dawn in January 1943, were rushed in buses with blinds down to Grand Central Station, and began a five-day train journey across Canada to the Rockies. I played chess all the way with Sydney Scroggie, a journalist from Dundee. Only one stop enlivened the journey over the endless snow-covered tundra. Our Second-in-Command, a Black Watch major called Wedderburn, rightly decided that we needed exercise, but wrongly decided to stop the train for it at Saskatoon without warning the citizens or asking their leave. It was a Sunday morning, and the good people of Saskatoon, on their way to church, were astounded by the sight and sound of six hundred soldiers, wearing rucksacks, running in threes down their main street and back again, with never a word to anyone. It was bizarrely discourteous.

In the Rockies, however, the snowbound townsfolk of Jasper made us very welcome. We were lodged in the comfortable cabins of the National Park, but soon dispersed to the Columbia Icefield and other high camps, to learn skiing and ice-climbing. As usual, B Squadron found itself isolated, at Maligne Lake. The cold was startling, but it was a dry, windless cold, and we suffered only when sleeping out in two-man tents without fires. I began to see how self-reliant the ex-crofters could be in harsh conditions. Some of our ski-instructors, however, were French Canadians from Quebec, which was a mistake. They were pro-Vichy, and had no enthusiasm for what we were doing or about to do to France. Anything related to the war was a taboo subject. More important, when I had to order 'no fires tonight' to simulate fighting conditions, the Quebecois lit a roaring fire in the forest a few yards away. *Vive Quebec libre.*

The local guides were different, good at rough, cold living and ready with useful advice. We learned not to expose our private parts too long; to take our boots into our sleeping-bags; to beware hidden logs when skiing in deep snow; to avoid snow-blindness. They showed us how to make snow-holes, and it was not their fault that our petrol stoves generated dangerous volumes of carbon monoxide. I was one of the casualties.

Among the English experts who were with us was Frank Smythe, but far from well; and we saw little of him. My troop had Bob Freese, who had only one kidney but made light of it. Learning to ski was hard work because there were no lifts in those days, and we had to climb every foot of the way, with loads. Trail-breaking in deep snow was so exhausting that the leader had to be relieved every quarter of an hour. But skiing in the moonlight on hard crust,

The Lovat Scouts on the Athabaska Glacier

Mt. Taygetus from Sparta
(Spring 1936)

high above the tree-line, was pure pleasure.

With the spring and the warm sun, avalanches began. A man was killed by one in another squadron. Four of my men were carried away by a slab avalanche not far above the tree-line, just in front of my own skis. But for the trees, which broke up the slabs and stopped the bodies, they would have been carried into a ravine and probably killed. As it was two of them had fractured ribs and legs. It took us three days to get the improvised stretchers back a few miles to the Athabaska Highway, and as our food supplies had been air-dropped in the wrong place we were very hungry, a bad thing to be in cold weather. The regimental historian, Leslie Melville, is misinformed about this incident - as he so often was when B Squadron was involved - and places us where the food was dropped. If only we had been.

Back in our comfortable base-camp at Jasper we waited for the order to rejoin the war in Europe. My superstitious Hebrideans found themselves in a chalet with sourceless nightly voices, almost human but inarticulate, which didn't cease until a black bear and her cubs emerged from the under-floor space after their long hibernation.

In Nova Scotia we waited for a troopship and another dash across the Atlantic. Arriving in Britain just after D-Day, we were sent to Aberdeen, again with maps of Norway. In summer it would have been a sanguinary campaign. As it was the 52nd Division, having trained in the Cairngorms, were sent into action at or below sea-level on the island of Walcheren. The Lovat Scouts, having trained for Arctic warfare, were given tropical kit and sent to Naples. One or two officers, mostly the climbing experts, disappeared. Only the two Norwegians came with us, to their cost. They had escaped from their country across the North Sea in a small boat, and were never to return home.

Slow as it was, the convoy was unmolested by submarines or

the Luftwaffe. We enlisted a returning prisoner-of-war, a Sicilian colonel, to teach us some Italian. Archie Turnbull, who could recite Dante, was the fastest learner, but acquired a Sicilian accent. By that time a deafness for consonants caused by my weapon training had begun to trouble me (only naval gunners used ear-plugs in those days), but Italian consists mainly of vowels, and I picked up enough to communicate with partisans in the Appennines.

The transit camp at Afragola, near Naples, was an introduction to the squalor that follows fighting. The village was out of bounds because of smallpox, venereal diseases and typhus (I think bubonic plague came later). The population was on the verge of starvation, and women and girls were being offered by their fathers or brothers in exchange for food or marketable cigarettes. We were soon on our way in trucks, however, to the Appennines and the Gothic Line. As we passed through the village of Cassino, below the high monastery, we stared at the blasted buildings and what looked like bundles of clothing in the alleys. Everyone had heard of the appalling casualties, but the sight was not good for our morale.

Whatever the purpose for which we had been trained, the 8th Army used us sensibly. It was concentrating for an attack through the low ground where the Appennines dip to the Adriatic, while the US 5th Army punched through the valleys near Bologna. That left a long mountain front very sparsely manned, although there were German and Austrian troops somewhere in there. We were to take the place of a much larger French mountain regiment which had been withdrawn to take part in the attack on the south of France. Our task was activities which would conceal the absence of real forces. We would have the services of some 25-pounder guns on a rota basis (in my own sector on Thursdays), but with limited ammunition. The partisans might help us with information They did when we ran into them occasionally, but their private agenda concentrated on local revenges.

The real war began at last as we disembarked from our three-ton trucks to eat. We must have been observed, because the shelling began almost at once. Only a few shells, bursting quite a distance behind us, but enough to loosen the bowels before we hastily moved on. The leading truck took a wrong turning as a result of bad map reading, and headed for the enemy. As we passed some Indian infantry we noticed that they were crouched in slit-trenches, and looked surprised to see us driving through their positions. Mysteriously the leading truck suddenly stopped, backed into a providential field, and came back fast. We did likewise, even faster. Fortunately the enemy gunners reacted slowly, and we left without casualties.

My squadron was to take over a densely wooded hill from a Gurkha company, and I was detailed to spend the night with them in order to get some idea of how these experienced troops held the position. An English captain led me round. It was pitch dark long before we had finished, and what struck me was the Gurkhas' silent invisibility. Whenever we stopped in the trees it was because the captain had been soundlessly halted by two kukris, held at shoulder level, and I would find another behind me. The Gurkhas' penchant for nocturnal decapitation was legendary.

At daybreak B Squadron took over. Another squadron were made less welcome on the next mountain. Steel helmets being too heavy and conspicuous, we had been equipped with khaki forage caps rather like baseball caps, instead of our distinctive dark blue bonnets. Unfortunately they were also rather like the enemy's grey forage caps, and at a distance colours are not so distinguishable. So C Squadron were shot at by the Gurkhas. Luckily most shooting in mountains is inaccurate because the target is further away than usual, and at a different level, so that the lesson was bloodless one. Forage caps were quickly replaced by balaclavas.

As in Canada B Squadron's position was separated from the

main regiment's. Our first night on the hill was a jumpy one. I had ordered 'nothing up the spout' (i.e. no cartridge in the breech), but the troop next door shot one of their own men as he came back in the dark from a pee in the bushes. Simon had to read the burial service next morning. We dug ourselves in as best we could in rather shallow soil, in places not chosen by the Gurkhas. When the enemy is at a distance - in this case on the other side of a valley - the sensible place for slit-trenches is just below the crest of the hill on one's own side, so that the enemy can't be sure exactly where one is or where his shells are landing. As we moved from hill-top to hill-top we learned how to make our positions unobtrusive. This did not suit the regiment's second-in-command, the Black Watch major called Wedderburn, when he arrived to inspect us. Famous for having dropped bombs by hand from an aircraft in the Spanish civil war, he felt that the Scouts - or at least B Squadron - lacked enthusiasm. He would insist that he and I stride visibly along the crest of the hill, no doubt to emphasise our presence to the Austrians. The shells did not start coming until he had left, and since the men discussed his antics in Gaelic I was not obliged to reprimand them.

A godly American once said that there are no atheists in fox-holes. I did not experience any spiritual conversion, and would have been ashamed if I had. All I believed in then, and later, was luck. Not that our positions were ever shelled or mortared heavily, in spite of Wedderburn's exhibitionism. The Appennine thunderstorms, however, were almost as frightening. We could see them coming up the valley from the Arno. When the rifles and tommy-guns started hissing we would put them out of the trenches and cower under our ground sheets. There would be a few flashes of lightning, a few ear-splitting cracks, and sheets of rain, followed by enough sunshine to let us dry out before dark.

The order soon came down from the hyperactive Wedderburn

that Simon was to send out a small patrol with the object of establishing a radio behind the Austrian positions, from which information could be relayed about targets such as supply dumps. The choice lay between me and Alasdair Urquhart, a repertory actor with whom I shared many jokes about our seniors (he survived the Italian campaign only to die of pneumonia in a pantomime). My troop was chosen. The project did not appeal. We had only a vague notion of the Austrian positions, and our Italian maps were notoriously inaccurate. The fact that Wedderburn's order had not specified any time-limits suggested that his real intention was to find out where the Austrians were by provoking some sort of encounter. If so, he succeeded.

I surveyed the wooded valley through Simon's stalking telescope, having discarded mine as a cumbersome luxury. I wrote a letter to my wife, chose a corporal, four riflemen and a radio operator, and waited for dark, wishing I had not forfeited the right to pray. We set off down into the trees in single file, myself in front with a tommy-gun, because I had some idea of where we were supposed to go. For the rest of the men the order was 'nothing up the spout', as I did not fancy being shot in the back. The deeper we got in the valley the thicker the brambles became - Appennine brambles are notorious - until we could not get through without making a dangerous amount of noise. When we came across a cart-track that seemed to be pointing in the right direction I decided to use it, as we now had rubber-soled mountain boots, much less noisy than nailed ones on stony ground. After a mile or so the track dipped, and we began to hear the purling of a stream. It was still pitch dark.

Suddenly there was a shout from ahead and a burst of submachine-gun fire. As we threw ourselves down I cocked the tommy-gun and fired in the direction of the flashes - a completely instinctive action preceded by no mental event that could be called a decision, as Gilbert Ryle would have said. Feet could be heard stumbling down the stream. There followed a long, tense silence. Everyone had gone to ground, and was relishing the darkness. After what must have been at least ten minutes my corporal appeared soundlessly at my elbow, and we crawled forward. There was a body lying in the stream, still warm, with a Schmeisser beside him. We collected the rest of the patrol, except for the radio operator, who was missing. While the corporal and I kept alert for more activity a rifleman searched the body, and found papers which yielded a little information next day.

It seemed to me that there was no point in taking the patrol further. Having lost the radio we could not do what the patrol was - ostensibly at least - meant to do; and this valley was evidently in use by the enemy. After a long wait for daylight - in case we were shot by our own people in the dark - we climbed back up to our hilltop position. The radio operator had already done so, luckily without getting shot. It turned out that the man I had killed was a young Austrian mountain infantry man, coming down from his hilltop to go on leave. Either he and his companion had taken a wrong turning or his base was further down the valley.

Although we had at least gained this bit of information, Wedderburn told Simon that I should have persevered with the patrol. Perhaps he had not been told that our radio operator had disappeared. Simon was kinder when he discussed the incident with me. The fact that I was the first in the squadron to kill one of the enemy would enhance my reputation with the men, he said, and I must not feel guilty about the killing (I didn't, but it was nice of him to think I might). The result, however, was to make me regard Wedderburn as disingenuous as well as foolhardy. Ironically it was foolhardiness, not useful courage, that eventually killed him. On leave at Christmas he fell to his death while sliding down the marble banisters of a hotel, a sad end for a well-known rock-climber. I don't know what his kin were told, and I have hesitated to record what I was told; but anyone who might have cared must be dead by now.

Before that, however, my squadron had moved to Milton's leafy Vallombrosa. We were always moving from hill to hill, with an occasional night of rest down near the Arno. My second patrol - ordered by the restless Wedderburn again - was intended to find an Austrian and take him prisoner for interrogation. 'Rather you than me' said Alasdair again. I had assumed that it would again be a night patrol; but no, it was to start in daylight, not even Simon could explain why. Perhaps my previous performance in the dark had failed to impress; but my guess was that Wedderburn wanted more shooting. If so, he got it.

After several hours of stalking in the vineyards around Borgo alla Colline we spotted - and must have been spotted by - a soldier in a house beyond the village walls. As we crossed the road towards this building several grenades were thrown at us, and we dived into the ditch. A Spandau machine-gun opened up, and we crawled back towards the village by way of the ditch. To get into the shelter of the buildings we had to dash a few yards in front of a wall which the Spandau was spraying. My sniper, Macleod, shouted that he could see the machine-gunner through his telescopic sight, and shot him. The brief silence allowed most of the patrol to get into the village, leaving Macleod and me. As Macleod fired again I made my dash, the Spandau started up again, and I could see the bullets hitting the wall stomach-high. Macleod later said that his bullet made the second machine-gunner rear up from his window-sill, so that the Spandau dipped. The bullet that hit me penetrated my calf instead of my guts, and the firing ceased. Manning the Spandau must have become unpopular, and during the brief silence Macleod joined us in shelter, having saved the patrol from serious casualties. I was hobbling with difficulty and told the patrol to leave me (the Austrian *Gebirgsjäger* treated prisoners decently), but they dragged me through Borgo until an elderly peasant offered us not only his donkey but his guidance through the woods. It was a brave offer that would probably have cost him his life if the Austrians had caught him. They were mortaring us now, rather vaguely, but we were soon in the woods. The peasant seemed to have a remarkably precise notion of where our slit-trenches were, and I had an easy ride. Back in our position I tried to reward him with money and food; but he sensibly refused them. Either would have betrayed him if he had been stopped by the enemy.

They were ruthless with civilians who helped us. The Italian partisans were sometimes ruthless too. Occasionally we met them in the hills, once with two soldiers, Austrian or German, whom they had found asleep. We were not at all sure what they intended to do with them, so we took charge of them in exchange for cans of meat. Another group of *partigiani* invited me down to a village to witness their 'trial' of a Fascist mayor. Thank goodness I was not in a position to accept. If I had been I would probably have had to witness a summary execution without being able to stop it.

My wound got me whisked by jeep down to a hospital near Arezzo, where the hole was probed and cleaned. My wife got a reassuring telegram the next day, but never the letter in which I recounted the drama, although I cannot imagine what use the information would have been to General Kesselring. I convalesced in Mussolini's magnificent Exhibition building at Ostia, where the stairs were made of glass and the plumbing was too delicate for human use. After physiotherapy I was given a dead man's boots for a trial walk, but my calf muscle was still too tender. The medical board which downgraded me asked me how I had got my wound. My reply was 'running away', but this was not the correct thing to say back in Rome, and eventually we settled for 'escaping an ambush'.

I felt guilty but enormously relieved not to be sent back to the Gothic line. I had been proud to be with the Scouts but like many of the junior officers felt that our seniors had - at that stage anyway - no personal experience of the sort of enterprises to which they were committing us. Leslie Melville put it more tactfully when he wrote in his book "It was a campaign ... in which the ability of junior leaders was of crucial importance". And sometimes our lack of experience, too. It was certainly the junior officers and NCOs who were our casualties. Lieutenant Tingulstad, my favourite Norwegian, was killed on another patrol with my men.

While convalescing at Ostia I was conscripted to be a member of a courts martial for the day. Our cases were trivial, but I remember one of them. An army cook had compassionately given a small amount of meat to an Italian woman with a child. He was court-martialled because there was a lot of black market trafficking in food between the Forces and civilians. As junior officer I was asked first for my proposed sentence, and because the amount of meat had been small and there had been no evidence that the woman had offered anything in return, I said 'simply admonish'. The presiding major - later a well-known name at the Bar - was outraged. Of course the cook was trafficking, and must get six months' detention, and so he did. Recalling my experiences of courts-martial (and courts of inquiry) years later, as a member of the *Criminal Law Review's* editorial board, I urged that we should commission an article or two on the subject, but was laughed at. It was many years before the Court of Appeal criticised the way in which courts-martial approached sentencing.

At Ostia I also got into financial trouble. I had the sense not to play poker, but thought I could hold my own at bridge, and couldn't. This was the only occasion on which I asked my father for money, and as he was in Bombay I had only a faint hope that he could help, or indeed that my letter would reach him. I never heard exactly what he did. It wasn't orthodox, because within a week or two a brown envelope containing a substantial bundle of *lire* was delivered to me in the camp by a messenger whom the guard could describe only as 'an Eyeteye'. One of my father's partners was a Gujerati, able to use the Gujerati underground which dealt in money by word of mouth across and between continents.

I spent the last few months of the war as a 'staff captain' at Allied Force Headquarters near Caserta, better paid but dealing with boring problems. My only non-trivial job was devising a points scheme for determining the order in which members of the South African forces should be repatriated. It worked acceptably, but involved me in involuntary corruption. Two South African officers who had become eligible for repatriation turned up in my office to ask me to get them a place on the next ship from Bari. I explained that I had no say in transport arrangements. They took some convincing, and when I was closing my office at the end of the day I found two bottles of whisky behind the door. Having no way of finding their owners I consumed them, and hoped that the donors would receive their deserts at Bari. Since I had granted no favour, and made clear that I could not, was this really corrupt? It was a question which a colleague of mine was to raise many years later, only to get a disastrous answer.

V.E. day came, though not in time to save my friend Sydney Scroggie from treading on a shoe-mine. It blinded him and shattered one leg below the knee, but he survived, married a St Dunstan's nurse, and eventually got a job in his home town, Dundee. Being a keen rock-climber he got friends to guide him up routes in the Cairngorms, although at times his artificial leg would slip unpredictably. The great Winthrop Young carried on climbing with an artificial leg - and a very brave professional guide - but he wasn't blind. Fifty-three years later Sydney presided at the Lovat Scouts' reunion in Inverness.

The rest of my war was uneventful, and rather pleasant. I spent leaves at Amalfi, Capri and Ischia. With blind Scroggie I tried to find the Sibyl's base at Cumae, but didn't. I visited the solfatara at Pozzuoli, a safety-valve for Vesuvius. The guide who shepherded us round the bubbling pools of lava said that 'scientists agree that Pozzuoli can be overwhelmed by an eruption at any time, but not this afternoon'. A day or two earlier an American GI had lost a leg, which had slipped into a lava pool while he was photographing it.

The *mezzogiorno* was a lazy, corrupt land, especially as the war receded. One of our AFHQ colonels was caught trying to smuggle a jeep-load of NAAFI supplies back to England. People were slack about swallowing their Mepacrine, which was rumoured to cause impotence, and the result was malaria. I contracted a recurrent fever which was sometimes called malaria, sometimes sand-fly fever, and which occasionally afflicted me for years after the war. Eventually I was flown back to an Aldershot hospital after two years in Italy. In the same plane and ward was a Major Izatt, who turned out to be a cousin of friends of mine. He had spent four years in the Mediterranean without home leave, but had recently developed a numbness in one arm after a vaccination. My Aldershot consultant simply told me to go home on leave, and gave me a note for the Edinburgh Tropical Diseases Unit; but when Izatt came back from his consultant he was deadly white. He had been asked whether he planned to marry, and when he asked why was simply told 'Don't. You'll be dead within six months'. The young consultant was right, but unforgivably brutal.

In Edinburgh I was given nothing to do except 'take the tablets' from the Tropical Diseases Unit, though I paid a few visits to my department in St Andrew's House. When I was finally demobilised a few months later I wasn't asked to hand back anything, so I still have my American cold-weather sleeping-bag, which later served me well for years in places as different as the

Cairngorms and the Grand Canyon, where nights can be remarkably chilly. I kept my privately owned Luger until the police persuaded me to give it up, together with a box of grenades which I must have acquired at Dunbar. My leg-wound was dismissed as minor, which it was. My nerve-deafness - the result of bangs - was incurable, and eventually earned me a small pension.

Also incurable, but not pensionable, was guilt, of the kind now called 'survivor guilt'. Time and again during six years in the army I had survived as a result of nothing but caution and luck. Now and again I had nerved myself to do things, quickly, that today make my blood run cold, but from a sense of duty, not enthusiasm. Perhaps it was my duty to try to rejoin the Scouts in the Appennines; but enthusiasm was lacking. I deal with this guilt, not with complete success, by reminding myself that some of us avoided seeing any action at all and at least I had not been responsible for any of our casualties.

My picture of the Lovat Scouts has more warts in it than Leslie Melville's semi-official book; but regimental historians are expected to glorify. The Scouts' record in three wars deserves the credit he gives them. Things happen in every regiment, however, which are not quite fit for official histories, yet not so scandalous that they need to be hushed up. Leslie Melville's chapter on the regiment's time in the Faroes - when he was a junior officer - is much better than his chapter on the Appennines, which conveys no picture of the terrain or its inhabitants, and no hint of our daily preoccupations with food, water, shelter and safe sleep, let alone the sudden fierce exchanges with the enemy.

The most readable personal memoir to emerge from the Mediterranean theatre of war was *Popski's Private Army*. Popski - in civilian life Vladimir Peniakoff - operated near us in the Appennines, but his little army's most spectacular achievements had been sabotage behind Rommel's lines in the North African hills. His relationship with the Senussi was like Lawrence's with the Bedouin, but his picture of their virtues and failings is less romantic. Like Leslie Melville's, his book is out of print. Popski is a hero of mine because he admits to having been scared, unlike, for example, Tilman or Hunt. They courted danger - in war as well as mountains - and they talk about lucky escapes and prudent withdrawals from threatening situations; but I suspect that for them talking about fear was talking dirty. This makes their autobiographies not quite human. The books about the war-time army which I read for enjoyment now are the novels of Anthony Powell and Evelyn Waugh. Both saw how ridiculous and unfair the Army could be. If both share a fault it is snobbery about officers with plebeian backgrounds - Waugh's Hooper or Powell's Bithel, for example. Powell never saw what is called 'action', but Waugh did, and his courage under fire is well documented. It is a pity that *Sword of Honour* was so unkind to the unbrave - another sort of snobbery.

6. A LUCKY BUREAUCRAT

"The Way the Wind Blows"
(Lord Home's memoirs)

Back to the Scottish Office, as an Assistant Principal, junior to the contemporaries who had not left their desks, paid less than a staff captain, and worked much harder. Back too came George Pottinger, who had joined the Scottish Office in 1939 as I had, and turned out to have been one of our Thursday afternoon gunners in the Appennines. George was a dashing civil servant. He was one of the 'British Warm Brigade' who long after demobilisation wore the smart major's greatcoat known as a 'British Warm'. Another British Warm was Douglas Inch, our medical officer who founded the psychiatric clinic in Glasgow that was later named after him. Both he and Pottinger became members of the New Club rather earlier in their careers than was usual at St Andrew's House. George, a 'son of the manse' became well-known for his cultivation of wealthy businessmen, with consequences which nobody at the time foresaw.

Exotic newcomers had been recruited as Principals during or after the war. There were senior civil servants from India and the Sudan, men with experience and commonsense, now in junior posts. There was Maclehose, an ex-publisher who was said to have rejected *England, Their England*, only to see it become a best-seller. There was Callan Wilson, a Presbyterian missionary from Africa, who believed, like Nurse Cook, in predestination, and drove his car accordingly. Once, in the course of a long train journey, he tried to persuade me that *Revelations* foretold the Suez debacle of 1956.

It was nearly six months, however, before George Pottinger and I were made Principals. Meanwhile we had a lot to learn. I, for one, had to learn to write decent English. My grammar and spelling were as good as anyone's, but my vocabulary was poor, and the Army had not enriched it with any usable words. It is remarkable that my Christ Church tutors, who had read or listened to so many of my essays, had either not noticed this or forborne to point it out. My Principal, MacRobbie, did not forbear. Although he had left school at 16, and worked his way up the clerical and executive ladders, he had a feeling for English which many a don doesn't. He had a nose for imprecision, time and again pointing out that I had said what I could not mean, or had missed the *mot juste*. I was irked at the time, but grateful later. I came to value him as an elderly friend, and was grieved when he and his wife were killed in a car crash.

The Labour government were creating the National Health Service, and the Department of Health for Scotland was imitating almost every step taken by the Ministry of Health. The British Medical Association was driving hard bargains with Aneurin Bevan, who dared not alienate it. Cigar-smoking doctors with gold fountain-pens faced cautious ministers and civil servants across the negotiating table. Scotland dared not rock the boat. Because of the crofters' poverty we already had a health service of sorts in the Highlands and Islands Medical Service, but its doctors had never been unionised or money-minded, and all the hard bargains were now being driven in Whitehall. Indeed the doctors of the islands were another sort of problem at that time. Physicians with what are now called 'problems' tended to gravitate either to ships or to the Outer and Inner Hebrides. The Department of Health for Scotland had a medical officer whose responsibilities included visits to every doctor in the area to find out how heavily he was drinking and whether he was abusing the drugs he dispensed. In one island which I used to visit I was told by a housewife that she would never trust the local practitioner, but took her children all the way to Inverness.

My own responsibilities were the supply and pricing of drugs and glasses, and the pharmacists and opticians with whom I dealt were neither grasping nor delinquent. The most serious problem became clear only a day or two after NHS prescriptions began to flood into the central pricing bureau in Glasgow, which was failing to cope. Although it was an independent bureau it seemed to need advice, and I sent two of my experienced staff to advise, which speeded up the pricing. When the head of my division heard what I had done he pointed out the danger of interfering. If our interference hadn't saved the day the news media would have made our department the target for the blame. I had come across this self-protecting attitude at AFHQ in Caserta, but lost my temper.

I lost my temper a lot in those post-war days. We worked hard and late - usually taking work home to finish near midnight. Week-ends began on Saturday afternoons or Sundays. So many of our colleagues were middle-aged or elderly that the young Principals in politically sensitive departments were moved from job to job as political concerns changed. I myself had nine quite different jobs in 11 years, and was not given time to become really knowledgeable about any of them. By way of contrast my friend Ralph Law, in the peaceful and bucolic Department of Agriculture, was allowed to become the expert on the problems of the Highland and Islands, and sat in the same seat for those same eleven years, before falling dead on a golf-course.

As a Principal I spent a lot of my time writing reports for committees. Most of my chairmen were reasonable and skilful operators, especially Baillie Maclean of Paisley; but with the pettifogging chairman of the Scottish Building Costs Committee, Sir George Laidlaw, I lost my temper so completely that he asked the Department's deputy head to replace me. He did so, but told me he sympathised. I was much happier as secretary of the Scottish Housing Advisory Committee. One of our achievements was a report on the planning and design of houses for the elderly. It struck me that nobody seemed to have asked the elderly how they would like to be housed, and I was allowed to commission, and help to design, the first survey of its kind in the UK. It exploded the myth, for example, that most of the elderly wanted to be housed away from families with children, or that most preferred showers to baths. The report led to clever little additions to housing schemes which were the work of Mrs Blanco White, one of the Department's best architects.

Loss of temper was not my only problem. Anxieties and terrifying dreams were another. My wife persuaded me to go to a psychoanalyst. Fairbairn was interested in what would now be called 'post-traumatic stress disorder', and took on ex-servicemen at somewhat lower charges than most analysts. The originalities in his articles and his book already commanded respect, so much so that an analyst in the USA whose book I came across years later paid him the compliment of plagiarism. As a treater of patients he was not so outstanding, and rather difficult to like; but my symptoms abated. What was also of benefit was some sort of liberation from the ways of thought of Oxford, the Army and the civil service. He revived my prewar interests in psychology and philosophy, and Edinburgh University allowed me to begin a doctoral thesis on *The logical status of the Freudian unconscious*, a title which incurred much ridicule among my friends. Fairbairn doubted my ability to succeed - a doubt which as my analyst he should have kept to himself - but I was encouraged by my friend Peter Heath, a squash-playing philosophy lecturer, later a professor at Charlottesville. At first everything I wrote on the subject seemed inadequate, but I discovered an ancient typewriter of my late father-in-law's, and my typescript seemed to make more sense than my manuscript. This breakthrough led me to type my own minutes in the St Andrew's House files, instead of dictating them to a typist

- a habit which raised eyebrows, as if a doctor had soiled his hands with a bedpan.

I could not have finished my thesis, however, if I had still been running a branch in the Department. Fortunately I had been appointed private secretary to the Scottish Office's new Minister of State, the Earl of Home. The Secretary of State for Scotland, James Stuart, had created this post so that during his frequent and prolonged absences in Whitehall he would have a deputy in Scotland. Home, who as a prewar MP had been Parliamentary Private Secretary to Neville Chamberlain at the time of Munich, had gone to the Lords on his father's death, and so was much less often obliged to be at Westminster. While Parliament was sitting Cabinet and Commons business kept James Stuart in Whitehall from Monday to Thursday, but Home kept the shop open all week in Edinburgh, and could receive deputations at much shorter notice than the Secretary of State.

He was meant, too, to pay special attention to the neglected development of Scotland's rural and urban industries. As a landowner he could deal knowledgeably with farmers, and on friendly terms with forest owners. The Forestry Commission wanted them to plant more conifers, but on land with thin soils and high winds. The forest owners knew that this would mean investing capital with no prospect of quick returns and a risk of no returns at all. Accompanied by me and an expert from the Commission - by a coincidence Geoffrey Forrest who had been the Lovat Scouts' Adjutant - the Minister toured the north. The landowners received us hospitably. We got many a free lunch but planted few plantations. Home was equally unsuccessful with the western industrialists, who received him equally hospitably but were not going to risk their money on big new enterprises.

Expeditions to Glasgow were much less agreeable than our northern tours. They usually involved meeting the Provost of the city. One of them had just married or remarried at the age of 70, and his small-talk was full of broad hints about his restored virility. It was the custom at that time to hand out a knighthood to every Lord Provost of Glasgow, which became known as the City of Dreadful Knights.

I have hardly ever found politicians (or courtiers) likeable, but Home was one of the exceptions. He was good-humoured, kind to those who worked for him, and did not take problems too seriously - unless they really were serious. Unlike James Stuart, whose taciturnity was almost sinister, he would joke about the things he was expected to do - but do them well. He made no pretence that I was an equal: he called me 'Walker' and I called him 'Sir'. He was a patrician, and assumed that families like the Cecils were congenitally good at government. His reply when Wilson taunted him with being the 14th Earl was famous: 'Well, I suppose he is the 14th Mr Wilson'. Yet he would jocularly admit that he might well be the descendant of a French glass-blower. Scottish audiences were supposed to have heard of the Douglas Cause. In Boswell's time Lady Jane Douglas, who had not yet produced a child, returned with twins from a visit to Paris at the age of 50. Since one of the twins was the heir presumptive to a title and huge estates, their legitimacy was challenged by one of the Hamilton dynasty, who claimed that she had bought them from a glass-blower in France. The court gave the lady the benefit of the doubt, but Home regarded himself as lucky. Nor did he lose his sense of humour at work. An undersecretary who had a markedly receding chin had a long meeting with him about the licensing of bulls with undershot jaws, which was a genetic handicap for grazing animals. As the door closed behind him Home muttered 'If Campbell were a bull would we have to license him?'

One of the jobs of a minister's private secretary is to make sure that *Hansard* reports him accurately, and sometimes to make sure that it doesn't. Home, who spoke well, never gave me trouble, except over the occasional statistic. One private secretary, however, had to deal with a junior minister who had been defending some regulations at a late night sitting of the Commons. A member of the opposition taunted him with forgetting a promise made by Tom Johnston, the war-time Secretary of State. The minister lost his temper and said 'I don't give a bugger what Tom Johnston promised ...' In those days the *Hansard* editors were more open to negotiation than they are nowadays, and the minister's outburst was reported as 'Of course one must not lightly disregard the pledges of a predecessor.'

A less lucky private secretary had to tell a junior Scottish Office minister what he could not do. The minister had been invited by a newspaper from his constituency to write them an article on the current economic crisis. He was no economist, but that morning there landed on his desk a copy of a cabinet paper with a masterly overview of the situation. Delightedly he told his private secretary to have it retyped, without the SECRET label and the paragraph numbers, so that he could send it to the newspaper editor. The private secretary explained that this would be most improper, but it took the Permanent Secretary to dissuade the junior minister.

To have an unsatisfactory minister is the worst thing that can befall a department, and especially a private secretary. Alan Clark, in his famous Diaries, seems to reveal himself as quite unsuited to be even a parliamentary undersecretary. Disloyal to his Secretary of State, contemptuous of civil servants as an entire class, he was usually too lazy to read his briefs, and when he did read them often failed to grasp the points that they were making. When annoyed he used schoolboy epithets - 'spastic', 'fucking', 'cunt' - at meetings and dinner parties. Some of the diary's entries in 1990 betray a manic delusion of success. He intrigued constantly, at first in order to be Parliamentary Private Secretary to Mrs Thatcher, later in the hope of being made a Secretary of State; but she is said not to have trusted him. Even his hill-climbing, which would have redeemed him a little in my eyes, was competitive rather than done for enjoyment.

The only thing that disappointed Home's civil servants was his reluctance to take a tough line when it seemed that this might have gained a worthwhile objective. He was particularly apt to give way in the Lords. When legislation was afoot to update the statutes of the Scottish Universities one of its provisions was the abolition of Lord Rectors. These were elected by the students to represent their interests, and to chair the meetings they were expected to attend. The elections tended to produce comedians, journalists or worse, who accepted nomination for the sake of publicity, attended rarely and when they did attend usually made a mess of meetings. Yet Lord Crawford and Lord Reith made a fuss in the upper house about the ending of 'a fine tradition', and Home gave way, to the dismay of the Universities' Principals. Even within the walls of St Andrew's House Home would seldom argue with his political colleagues, and never with James Stuart, to whom of course he owed his job. Later, as his career took him far beyond the Scottish Office, I began to suspect that what we had regarded as weakness was really farsightedness. He called his autobiography *The Way the Wind Blows*, and I think the title was meant to be self-revealing.

What he never did was to treat his civil servants as servants. 'Do you think you could ...' was his way of giving an order, which reminded me of Simon Campbell-Orde sending me on patrols. He was considerate as well as well-mannered. He had been a first-class amateur cricketer, and would invite me to go with him to Lords until he sensed that it bored me. He gave my wife and me seats in the Abbey for the dress rehearsal of the coronation, where we witnessed the collapse of the aged Lyon King at Arms. The Homes would ask us down to their house at Springhill for weekends of mixed work and play. Lady Home was not only an invaluable support for a man whose physical strength seemed barely enough for his job. He had been incapacitated by spinal tuberculosis for most of the war, and frequently cancelled meetings because of illness. She was also a person of great understanding and kindness.

As Private Secretary I was often included in visits to the homes of the illustrious. Dunvegan was an example. Flora Macleod, the head of the clan, had refurbished it with financial help from clansmen all over the world, and invited the Minister of State, Lady Home and me to stay there when he opened Skye Week. We were of course shown the Fairy Flag, which used to save the Macleods from annihilation in battle, later from bankruptcy; but even more fascinating was Dame Flora's story about her great-uncle. He was of Viking descent, and when Norway was on the point of becoming independent of Sweden he was secretly asked to receive a deputation. To his astonishment they asked him whether he would consider accepting the Norwegian crown if it were offered to him. It was not quite clear from Dame Flora's account whether what was on offer was the crown, or merely a place on the short list.

When the Conservatives were returned to power in the early fifties ministers tended to assume that their civil servants had more sympathy with their Labour predecessors. Home shared this assumption, which was strengthened by a clash with the Department of Agriculture. Part of my job was scrutinising every one of the blue 'submissions' that came to him from the four Scottish Departments, looking especially at annexes and appendices in case he didn't. Only once did I detect a clear attempt to conceal something from him. It was the legal effect of a small but politically important clause in a Bill, relating to 'tied houses', and the Department had hoped that he wouldn't notice it. When I pointed it out to him, there was a first-class row. One result was that he trusted his 'private office', but not the Department of Agriculture.

It must have been about this time that I was invited to join the Speculative Society, Edinburgh's equivalent of the Twenty Club at the House. When created in the nineteenth century it had been given rooms in the Old Quadrangle, and had managed to avoid eviction ever since. Every new member had to deliver a well-prepared paper, and a box in its library was found to contain Robert Louis Stevenson's. It was not, as I recall, of the quality one would have expected. We had it covered in watered silk by a prisoner at Perth, but took no other precautions. I wonder whether it is still there.

The Society's members were mostly young advocates, lecturers and writers. The advocates included Cameron the younger, who succeeded his father as Lord Justice Clerk, the equivalent of England's Lord Chief Justice. (His father was a member of a more frivolous society, the Monks of St Giles, where I later had a memorable encounter with him). Nicholas Fairbairn the advocate was the son of my psychoanalyst. Nicholas was at that time well-known as the fairly successful defender of Glasgow gangsters, sometimes criticised for his forensic tricks. His politics in those days involved gun-boats, and he was later to succeed Home as MP for Perth and Kinross. His debating style was aggressive, and his wit slightly coarse, as Parliament was to observe when he became Solicitor-General for Scotland - for a very short time. He had a romantic side, and not only painted landscapes but bought and skilfully restored Fordell Castle. Like so many advocates he drank heavily, but unlike most he died of it.

I recall witnessing about this time the spectacular effect of whisky on Thornton Wilder. I was the guest of Douglas Young at a Pen Club lunch, at which Thornton Wilder was the guest of honour. During lunch I watched Compton Mackenzie - known in Edinburgh as 'The Crofter of Drummond Square'- refill his glass with whisky not once but several times. When Wilder got up to deliver what was evidently a well-worn speech a strange thing happened. He made the gestures which were appropriate to each sentence, but a second late. The effect was that of a film whose sound-track has slipped.

I have a vivid memory of Home's promotion. Eden had just succeeded Churchill as Prime Minister. Home and I were driving back from a visit to Campbelltown when a police car flagged us down, with a message asking him to telephone Downing Street. There were no telephone kiosks on that lonely coast, but we came to a wayside inn. The only visible phone was in full view and hearing of the customers, who were all agog, but the owner admitted that he had a more private one in his bedroom which the Minister could use if he did his best not to wake the baby. I sat by the somnolent infant, rocking its cot occasionally, while Home and Eden shouted amicably at each other. Home was to take over the Commonwealth Office. It looked after him with less care than the Scottish Office. Our messengers used to place his racing bets for him - and often profited by following his knowledgeable choices; but the Commonwealth Office was too priggish for that sort of thing. Worse, when a newspaper accused him of having got a Fourth in history at Oxford the Commonwealth Office's public relations staff stupidly pointed out that he had got a Third. St Andrew's House would have had more sense.

The Commonwealth, however, was something that had really interested Home. Throughout his time at St Andrew's House he had taken a close interest in the fate of Rhodesia and South Africa. My guess now is that for him being Minister of State was merely an agreeable staging-post: 'great fun', he later called it when I met him at a Gaudy, but not a job to dedicate himself to. He preferred fishing the Tweed to anything the Scottish Office could offer, and many a time decided at the last minute that he was not well enough to leave Springhill. At the Commonwealth Office, and later the

Foreign Office, both of which involved him in extensive travels, his stamina seemed remarkable. Nor was he ever regarded in Scotland as a conceivable successor to Macmillan. He was a nice man, we thought, but not a leader. Having had enough of leaders I liked him.

7. A BORED BUREAUCRAT

"But I knew it was a shiver of joy ..."
(a witness of an execution)

Not long after his departure I was promoted and transferred to the Scottish Home Department - a lucky escape from the Department of Health, where promotion seemed limited to golfing friends of the Permanent Secretary, Douglas Haddow. Haddow had a First in mathematics from Cambridge, but told me - without the slightest shame - that he had chosen the subject only because it seemed his best chance of getting into the Civil Service.

In the much more congenial Scottish Home Department I was given the division responsible for juvenile delinquents. The Department was a small one, but its head was Charles Cunningham, a slave-driver who was later made Permanent Undersecretary of State at the Home Office. In St Andrews House he was admired and liked, but notorious for redrafting almost every document prepared by his subordinates, so that neither he nor his senior staff went home until late at night. Another foible was his trust in the advice of experts, even when his administrators had found them untrustworthy.

Nevertheless he was 'an artist of the possible', able to persuade the most difficult of ministers, and it was with surprise that we heard that in the Home Office his idiosyncrasies had made him intensely unpopular with both his subordinates and at least one Home Secretary. The contrast reminds me of Chenevix-Trench, who was such a success as headmaster of a small public school (Bradfield) but regarded as a disaster when he went to the much larger Eton. I knew him slightly, as he had been a fellow undergraduate at the House, before being taken prisoner by the Japanese and put to work on the 'Death Railway'. When I next met

74

him, skiing at Davos with some of his boys, he had strayed into deep snow and collapsed. I was skiing with a doctor from the Commandos, Jock Rushforth, who examined him and said that he was still showing the effects of malnutrition, years afterwards.

But I am talking about Charles Cunningham. He had made himself unpopular with Roy Jenkins, whose autobiography devotes no less than four pages to his insubordinations. At that time the Home Office had suffered a quick succession of Secretaries of State, each with his own pet innovations. In less than a decade Charles had to cope with four - Butler, Soskice, Brooke, and now Jenkins, for who knew how long. This one wanted not only to reorganise the place but also to import a private secretary from his old department. Worse, he objected to receiving only those 'submissions' which bore Charles' *imprimatur*, and wanted to know why he couldn't see any dissenting minutes by senior officials. The last of these issues struck at the core of Charles' principles. He felt personally responsible for any advice which his department gave to the Home Secretary. I had personal experience of this in the Scottish Home Department, but his minister, James Stuart, was too well-mannered - or not interested enough - to go behind Charles' back. After retiring from the Home Office Charles became Deputy Chairman of the Atomic Energy Authority, and thereafter efficiently organised the resettlement of the 15,000 Asians whom Idi Amin had expelled from Uganda. Jenkins' picture of him is distorted.

Back at St Andrew's House Charles had been interested in juvenile delinquents. So I expected him to be enthusiastic about the new English juvenile courts. But it was a time when economies were being demanded, and surprisingly he decided - without consulting anyone else - that Scotland, unlike England, could do without juvenile courts for a little longer. A result he could not have foreseen was that years later Scotland was free, without opposition from entrenched interests, to introduce a Scandinavian-type 'children's panel', which dealt less formally than the English juvenile courts with all but the gravest crimes.

At first we were lucky enough to have a fine Chief Inspector, Hewitson-Brown, with an eye like a hawk for cruelty or abuse in childrens' homes. Unfortunately he was succeeded by a promoted inspector from the Home Office, whose policy was that inspectors should be ambassadors rather than detectives. He was a good ambassador, popular with local officials; but this apparently meant giving every institution advance notice of visits of inspection. The result, if not the intention, was that nothing serious was found. One such inspection cleared a home about which we had received several worried letters from local families. For example the fire-buckets full of water were said to be used to drench bed-wetters. It was not until I ordered a 'without notice inspection' that the Chief Inspector had to put in an adverse report. He seemed to be better at adverse reports on his own colleagues, for example our professional who was responsible for the after-care of released lifers. He reported to me - on far from conclusive evidence - that this excellent man was having an extra-marital affair with a rural probation officer. The report was written with the intention that it would go to the head of the department, but I made him promise that he would leave me to deal with it, and keep his mouth shut. I told the man concerned what had been reported about him, but that I was not taking any official action. He was very silent. I let him read the report and burned it in front of him. Later, after I had left, I learned that the dissatisfied Chief Inspector had not kept his mouth shut, but had not succeeded in usurping responsibility for prisoners' after-care.

I was glad to be moved to take over the division responsible for the sentencing of adult criminals. Of course I knew nothing about criminal law, but administrators were supposed to be able to familiarise themselves with a subject - and its history - in the course of a week-end. (This was before the Fulton Committee emphasised that frequent moves did not make for efficiency.) I was lucky to have under me David Cowperthwaite, who had been a magistrate in Nigeria, and saved me from many a mistake.

One of our responsibilities was the supervision of released lifers. We relied to a considerable extent on the same excellent after-care officer, who specialised in this work. One of his cases illustrates our problems. A Ukrainian ex- soldier had settled down in Glasgow with a Scots wife, and so had several of his friends, who used to spend evenings at his home. The wife noticed that they would sometimes talk in their mother tongue, and suspected that they were discussing her. One night he hit on her head with a hammer, nearly killing her, and was found to be suffering from paranoid delusions about her fidelity - a not uncommon situation. What was uncommon was her determination to get him discharged from his mental hospital. She found him a job in Glasgow and persuaded the hospital to let him out to work daily. Eventually we agreed with the hospital that he could live at home; but the after-care officer told the wife to let him know instantly if her husband did anything unusual. One night she telephoned him at home, in great anxiety, because her husband had begun to talk to his friends in Ukrainian again. A posse went quickly to the house, and found a hammer under the marital pillows.

Hanging was still the automatic sentence for murder, although Scots law allowed a plea of diminished responsibility at a time when English law didn't. Even when the verdict was murder Cunningham - unlike the head of the Home Office, Frank Newsam - wanted every effort made in capital cases to find a reason which the Secretary of State for Scotland could accept for commuting the death sentence. It was a rule, said to have been laid down by Queen Victoria, that the Scottish Office must consult the Home Office about every capital sentence, but we were free not to share their view, and sometimes commuted death sentences which in England would have been carried out. Usually it was possible to recommend commutation for one of the standard reasons: youth, for example, mental illness, or a 'scintilla of doubt' about guilt, which could be even fainter than 'reasonable doubt'.

A special case which I remember vividly was that of Ginger Forbes, a young seaman who had burgled a warehouse and beaten the night-watchman to death. He hadn't offered an insanity defence. It was routine for the condemned man to be interviewed by psychiatrists, since there was a common-law rule that a man must not be hanged if his wits are disordered (various odd reasons for this old rule are offered by old authorities who were probably guessing). Our psychiatrists reported that Forbes was neither mentally ill nor of low intelligence, but 'psychopathic'. This was a psychiatric diagnosis recently popularised by Sir David Henderson, the Edinburgh psychiatrist, and one form of it involved inability to control aggression. It was the only reason we could find for not hanging him, and the Home Office said that they would not regard it as sufficient. Cowperthwaite and I, however, based our memorandum on it. Cunningham managed to persuade the Secretary of State to advise the Queen accordingly, and she was obliged to commute the death sentence to 'life'. This was probably the only case in which 'psychopathy' alone has saved a murderer from the gallows in Britain. A year or two later, on a visit to Peterhead Prison, I saw Ginger Forbes for the first and last time; but there was an unfortunate sequel. After ten years (the standard period for reprieved murderers at that time) he was released on licence (not at my instance). After two months of freedom he stabbed two young men in a brawl outside a pub, and one died. By this time he was a 'mature' 33, so perhaps this vindicated the psychiatrists' view that his self-control was constitutionally weak.

Thirty years later he was released again, amid protests. He was 63, and said to be frail. One hopes very frail.

The only murderer whom we did not save from the gallows in my time was Peter Manuel, the notorious serial rapist and killer of his victims. He might conceivably have been diagnosed as psychopathic if he had not, after a minor fall, faked a sudden inability to talk or communicate. The psychiatrists tried to interview him, but could not, and were convinced that he was faking the disorder. The night before he was executed he ceased to pretend, and broke his silence; but was hanged.

The grimmest story about an execution was told to me by a senior prison officer who had been on the 'death watch' with a condemned man, during the weeks before his execution. The officer was deeply religious, and at last induced the man to pray with him, until he was confident of a conversion. As the murderer stepped into the execution chamber it was the Sheriff's duty to place a hand on his shoulder, and ask 'Are you [John Smith]?' in case he was the wrong man, as indeed he might have been in the old days of crowded gaols. The officer said that when this happened he saw the prisoner shiver. 'Everyone else thought it was a shiver of fear, but I knew that it was a shiver of joy that he was going to meet his Maker.' I think that the officer who told me this was trying to justify capital punishment. There was no doubt that this was the intention of the Bishop of Durham who in 1962 told a convocation about his experience with a condemned man:

> "Then began, in ... less than a week, the most wonderful reclamation and conversion that I have ever seen ... If ever I have seen a man fit for his Maker and for all eternity, it was that man. If he had been given a life sentence ... no conversion might well have occurred ..."

Emotionally I was seriously disturbed by hangings, and had nightmares in which I was the condemned man. When I was rational I felt no more uncomfortable about Peter Manuel than about the young Austrian mountain-trooper, for whom I had at least felt sorry. If one's philosophy of punishment is retributive, some offenders deserve death. If one is a utilitarian, there are some offenders of whom society is well rid. It can of course be rid of them without killing them. The argument that death is a more effective deterrent is now discredited, at least when homicides are concerned. There is plenty of evidence that the prospect of long incarceration is as effective as death in deterring lethal violence (although it may be more effective against other types of crime, such as drug-trafficking, for all we know). This leaves two arguments against executions for homicide. One is the possibility of a mistaken conviction: hence the British rule that if there was a 'scintilla of doubt' the death sentence should be commuted. The frequency of mistakes is exaggerated nowadays as a result of convictions which are quashed as 'unsafe', which doesn't mean mistaken - merely that the appellate court sees room for reasonable doubt about guilt. In any case there are some murderers whose guilt is undeniable, and their acts inexcusable. The argument based on mistakes implies that if a mistake can be ruled out the death penalty is morally tolerable. The stronger argument against it appeals to humanity. It is inhumane, according to the Privy Council, to keep a person under a death sentence for more than three years. Some people felt that the death penalty degrades our human nature even when as swiftly carried out as it was in Britain.

A decision which shocked us in the Scottish Office was the Home Secretary's refusal to commute Bentley's death sentence. Bentley and Craig were trapped by police on the roof of a building in the course of a burglary. Craig had a pistol, and shot a policeman fatally. He was under the minimum age for hanging (18), but

Bentley wasn't, and at his trial police said that he had shouted 'Let him have it' to Craig. He was convicted of murder, and the Home Secretary (Maxwell Fyfe, later Earl Kilmuir) let him hang. In Scotland Cunningham would have been able to prevent this. There was more than a scintilla of doubt as to what Bentley had meant by 'Let him have it'; but technically he was guilty anyway because he had known that Craig had armed himself with a firearm. In his autobiography Maxwell Fyfe tried to justify his decision on the ground that killing policemen is particularly to be discouraged. At the time we blamed Newsam, the permanent head of the Home Office, who was more reluctant than Cunningham to interfere with death sentences. It was not until many years later that another Home Secretary, Kenneth Clarke, made an unprecedented disclosure to the Commons - that Maxwell Fyfe had been advised by his civil servants not to let Bentley be hanged, but had overridden them.

A year or two after I had - inevitably - been moved to another 'hot seat' I found myself sitting opposite Lord Cameron, the head of the Scottish judiciary, at a dinner of the Monks of St Giles, a society in which local dignitaries meet in cowls to amuse each other. I was merely a guest. The wine had flowed, and Cameron began to abuse me loudly for commuting the death sentence of a lighthouse-keeper called Dickson. With half a dozen monks listening on either side of us I had to think quickly. Since he was really abusing the Department it didn't seem relevant to say 'it wasn't me', so I could only remind him that he should be saying all this to the Secretary of State. The next time I met him he seemed to have forgotten the matter. I doubt whether a scene of that sort could have taken place in London; but was any real harm done ? And in Scotland a man who 'has drink taken' is regarded as only partly responsible.

Less pardonable was the behaviour of another judge, Lord

Wheatley. I had found him an excellent chairman when I was secretary of one of his committees, but was shocked - as was most of the Scottish Bar - by his handling of the Argyll divorce. The law prohibited the news media from reporting the evidence in such cases; but Wheatley was so outraged by the details of the Duchess' infidelities that he circumvented this protection by recounting many of the details in his published judgment, which took three hours to deliver. It sold well as a commercial paperback.

To return to the Royal Prerogative of Mercy: it was not only used to commute death sentences. Every few months we had to send the Palace a beautiful but archaic document to enable Her Majesty to remit a borstal boy's unpaid fines. Since it was settled policy that nobody should leave borstal with a fine hanging over him it was high time that a simple clause to this effect was included in legislation; but it was many years before that happened. A more unusual use of the Prerogative was solemnly proposed by a salmon-poacher's solicitor. The sheriff had used his power to confiscate all the equipment involved, which included a car borrowed, not owned, by the defendant. We were asked to seek the Queen's mercy for an Austin Seven. We didn't.

What we did sometimes do was interfere with prison sentences. I particularly remember an elderly cobbler whose younger wife had left him for a younger man, living only a street away. He tried to persuade her to return, ending with threats to kill her if she didn't. One evening he was seen sharpening a knife on the window-sill of his tenement home, telling witnesses that this was the knife with which he was going to kill her. Nobody seems to have restrained him, or warned her, and he did. His defence was provocation, but the judge correctly instructed the jury that the obvious premeditation ruled that out in law. The jury thought differently, and convicted him of culpable homicide, not murder. The irritated judge passed a very long sentence of 15 years, to ensure that he was detained as long as if he had been convicted of murder but spared hanging. We used the Prerogative not to commute the sentence but to release him before he had served the statutory two thirds. This still seems to me the sort of case in which the jury system, whatever its shortcomings, has its uses, among which is the correction of excessive rigidity in the law. Almost exactly the same thing happened in an English case which the judge discussed with me (after passing sentence). The accused had married a woman who was 'on the game' but who gave it up to marry him. When he lost his job and had to seek work up north she went back to prostitution. When he found out they had a long argument in a pub, and parted. He went home and got the knife with which he killed her an hour or so later. Mr Justice Eveleigh had to tell the jury that since there had been 'cooling time' the defence could not be provocation; but the jury accepted the defence and found the man guilty of manslaughter, not murder. Unlike the Scottish judge Eveleigh felt he must respect the jury's decision, and gave the man only eight years.

Those were the days when the Wolfenden Committee was inquiring into the operation of the law relating to prostitution and homosexual acts. Its remit included Scotland, and it 'took evidence' from several witnesses in Edinburgh. I was not present, but I was told by someone who was that the chief constable of a large Scottish city denied that it had any prostitutes. I have always thought that when committees talk of the 'evidence' they receive they must be using the word in a more poetic sense than scientists or lawyers. 'Witnesses' tell committees what they would like to be the truth, and nobody talks of perjury.

Near the end of my time at St Andrew's House, the Vassall affair was blighting the careers of two people who had been friends of mine. Vassall, a junior civil servant in the Admiralty, was homosexual, and had been blackmailed into giving information to

Soviet agents. He had worked for Tam Galbraith, a likeable contemporary of mine at Christ Church, who had been a doggedly witty member of the Twenty Club, and was now a doggedly serious MP and a Civil Lord at the Admiralty. He seems to have been on friendly terms with Vassall - as he probably was with his other civil servants - and letters from him to Vassall were found, dealing with matters which were not official - for example one of Vassall's parties. Unfortunately some of these otherwise innocuous letters began 'My dear Vassall'. It was a not uncommon form of address in letters between senior civil servants, but not between ministers and junior clerks. (One by-product of the scandal was a Downing Street warning to ministers and civil servants about such endearments.) Some tabloid newspapers made the most of it, leading to successful libel suits by Tam. By this time he was a junior Scottish Office minister, but resigned when Vassall was convicted. The Radcliffe Tribunal on the Vassall affair exonerated him of any suspicions of carelessness or impropriety, and he was made a junior minister in a Whitehall department. He was knighted in January 1982, a few days before his premature death.

A more serious casualty was a colleague in the Scottish Office with whom I had often shared a tent and climbing rope without realising that he was homosexual. His career had taken him to London, where he lived with a male partner, and he had been a guest at more than one of Vassall's gay parties. Although nobody who knew him believed that this very professional man could be a security risk his promotion was cancelled just as it was about to be announced, since he was labelled unfit to be shown top secret documents. Unlike Tam Galbraith he couldn't sue anyone.

By the time Tam Galbraith arrived at the Scottish Office I was leaving it. In no more than eleven years I had been in nine different seats, some of them with several quite different responsibilities. I had coped with a dozen unrelated subjects without making any disastrous mistakes, but without achieving anything important that wouldn't have happened anyway, sooner or later. I knew that I would never be more than a mediocre civil servant, and the prospect of spending a quarter of a century in St Andrew's House was grim. As a senior civil servant I could ask for a sabbatical year, although Cunningham made me wait for it. But that year, and its sequels, belong to the next chapter.

The last Edinburgh house we lived in was typical of the South Side. Built of stone, standing on rock, it looked across a shallow valley to Marmion's Blackford Hill. When we left we sold it to a senior judge, the only one I have ever met whose conversation sounded like a nineteenth-century summing-up. He once said to me 'I cannot charge my memory with that'. Living now in an English house of post-war brick, floating on mud, I miss the solidity of Edinburgh homes and the variety of Edinburgh views. Cambridgeshire country gardens are lush, but one can be enclosed by too much chlorophyll, and the county has only one kind of view. Lovers of East Anglia talk instead of the enormous sky; but they are simply making the best of an absence of hills. Fenmen have no difficulty in believing that the earth is flat, whatever is said to happen west of the A1.

8. A LUCKY SABBATICAL

"Nouvelle Histoire ..."
(a French publisher's unauthorised title)

My first attempt to get a sabbatical research post was made at Manchester, which offered what was called the Simon Fellowship for civil servants and suchlike who wanted to do research of practical value. I can't remember what I proposed, but it led to a long interview with half a dozen professors and lecturers. There may have been other candidates, but I didn't see any. It was a bizarre interview, because when I asked what funds I could expect for my research they began to argue with each other, letting drop the fact that one of the departments involved had hoped to draw on the funds for some other purpose. The argument was not long, but as a spectator I got the impression that I might find myself playing a financial 'pig in the middle'. The impression was not improved when the chairman, who had suggested that I dine with him before catching my train, withdrew the invitation, saying that his wife had suggested that I would prefer to look around the centre of the city on my own. I had a solitary meal in a depressing hotel. When he telephoned that evening to offer me the fellowship I declined it. He was entitled to be irritated, but not to be surprised.

The Manchester fiasco was, in disguise, the luckiest vicissitude of my career, unless you count my leg-wound. Next year I applied to Nuffield College at Oxford for a similar one-year fellowship. This time there was certainly competition, but by this time I had published not only several official reports but also *A Short History of Psychotherapy*. Routledge had heard of my thesis, and suggested that I write the book. I had been quite keen to approach the subject in an unorthodox way, trying, in non-technical language, to relate psychotherapists' theories to what they actually did with their patients. My own analysis with Fairbairn had shown me that one could not have guessed from his writings what sessions with him would be like. I was of course accused by analysts of oversimplifying, and the book was more popular in translations than in English. Fifteen years after it appeared a French publisher produced a translation embarrassingly titled - without my permission - *Nouvelle Histoire de la Psychotherapie*.

Nuffield awarded me the fellowship. My project was to compare the morale of desk-workers in the civil service and in private firms. I was able to persuade two large government departments and two large firms in London to let me administer questionnaires to their staffs, and to interview samples, all under a pledge of anonymity which I still feel bound to honour. The survey I had commissioned for the Scottish Housing Advisory Committee had taught me quite a lot about the design of questionnaires, but I was surprised to find that nobody at Nuffield had any experience in the technique, although several fellows later adopted this approach. In those days a major problem was processing the data from large numbers of questionnaires. Norman Chester, the Warden of Nuffield, was able to persuade Harwell to use its newish computer for the purpose, and I shall for ever be grateful to the Harwell expert called Hailstone who did most of the work. His task was made no easier by the thunderstorms of July 1959, which triggered the valves in his machine, producing nonsensical figures. I hope he got whatever reward Chester's deal had secretly promised him. *Morale in the Civil Service* was the result of a hectic but satisfying year. It would be tedious to detail all my findings; but two are worth mention. Women in the civil service were much more enthusiastic about their prospects of promotion than their counterparts in firms. The latter saw a 'glass ceiling' not far above them, whereas the civil servants knew that at least one woman - Evelyn Sharp - had reached the top. Another finding was that the military notion that superiors should take an interest in the families and leisure activities of their subordinates was violently rejected by my office-workers, who valued their privacy. The English office culture was very different from the village that was St Andrew's House.

Supervisors' lack of familiarity with their subordinates was sharply illustrated by a woman in one of the sub-samples whom I interviewed. She was very paranoid, and suffered from what must have been delusions of persecution. Clearly she could have benefitted from treatment, for she was very unhappy. I had talked to personnel officers about the members of my sub-sample *before* interviewing them, and was given no impression that any of them were regarded as abnormal. This is a dilemma which often confronts research workers, especially in prisons, when they come across someone who needs help but can get it only if the researcher breaches confidentiality. I have known researchers who did breach confidentiality when it was clearly in the subject's interest to do so. For all I knew, however, this middle-aged woman was working satisfactorily and might well go on doing so. Paranoia - as I was to notice in academe as well as the civil service - is not always disabling.

What that research also confirmed was that there is no such thing as morale. Like a conglomerate rock it is a name for a collection of things: belief in the value (or uselessness) of what one is doing, belief that it is valued (or not) by others, optimism or pessimism about one's own career, acceptance or non-acceptance of the rules (about such things as sick-leave, bribes and perquisites), and solidarity - or its opposite - with colleagues. My own experience in the army and St Andrew's House had taught me that one's scores on these scales could not only vary but be quite independent of each other. One could believe in what one was doing, yet believe that hardly anyone else did, and that one would never receive one's deserts.

My sabbatical was also a pleasant and educative year. Nuffield had been founded by the motor-car millionaire as a college for graduates, although he came to regret it because of the left-wing reputation of its first fellows. The living conditions and other amenities which it offered graduate students were so much better than other colleges' that competition for one of its postgraduate places was intense. Architecturally, however, it was a joke, especially the tower on which the founder had insisted. Installing the library in the tower added to the joke, because it had half-a-dozen floors of rather limited capacity, so that users spent most of their time climbing stairs or waiting for the lift. The college's architectural secret , however, was that its proximity to the city sewer had made possible a heat exchanger which contributed to the warmth of the place.

The college specialised at first in politics and economics, but later appointed fellows who were sociologists (Jean Floud and Chelly Halsey for example) and modern historians (such as Freddie Madden). Since most of the postgraduate students were working for a D.Phil. under fairly intense supervision from the fellows the place was sometimes called a thesis-factory; but it was more than that. Norman Chester, its Warden, wanted it to be a link between Oxford and government. Politicians, heads of Whitehall departments, journalists were offered - and usually accepted - 'visiting fellowships' on the understanding that they would give and take part in private seminars. One met Callaghan, Heath, Dunnett (of the War Office, the older brother of my friend Denzil), Lawson (the elder), Robert Mark (Commissioner of the Metropolitan Police). Not all were as interesting and indiscreet as we had hoped: most were too experienced. One of them - I can't recall which - did betray some minor Government secret at dinner, and complained when it appeared in a Sunday newspaper. He had assumed, he said, that that there was a code of conduct which protected the confidentiality of what was said at an Oxford High Table. He was out of date.

Chester's cultivation of Whitehall was so assiduous that he began to go native, and wear a bowler hat for his trips to London. It was some time before he realised that in modern Whitehall bowler hats were worn not by mandarins but by off-duty Guards officers. The bowler vanished. Although I could never take him quite seriously as a college head, I discovered that others could fear him. To illustrate this I have to explain that among the many regrettable features of the college's architecture was a stretch of water in the lower quadrangle. Since it was a strict rectangle, about forty yards by six, it looked like a sawn-off canal. It was just deep enough to swim in, and at the end of a vinous summer party I urged Hugh Clegg, a tenured fellow, and Ruth Butterworth, an athletic student, to race each other down it. I went to bed, and it was only next day that Hugh came to tell me that they had done as I suggested, and that Chester was furious. Would I please tell him that it was my idea ? Ruth Butterworth, as a mere student, might have had reason to worry about her career, but Hugh's was already successful, and Chester could not have dislodged him even if he had wanted to.

That was later, however. He was anxious that this sabbatical fellowship of mine should become a popular one in Whitehall, as indeed it did. The official fellows took trouble to make me feel welcome. David Butler, the psephologist, became a friend who kept in touch for many years. I remember his taking me into dinner in Hall on my first night, explaining that the fellows hadn't yet decided whether their tradition was to remain standing until grace or to sit down and rise for grace. (David's amazing loyalty to Nuffield made him refuse several offers of chairs elsewhere, and he never left the college.) The college was rich, and raised no questions about the funds I needed for my research. The seminars in which fellows or students talked about research in progress were for me a new education in the social sciences.

I even made a tiny personal breakthrough in statistics. My sisters were gifted mathematicians, and taught their specialisms at universities; but at school I had been allowed to abandon the subject when I was having difficulty with the binomial theorem. Ten years later, convalescing from my wound in Rome, I had come across a book called *Mathematics for the Million* which encouraged me to think that - like my gifted sisters - I could cope with the subject. Nevertheless in Chapter 4 the fog got thicker and thicker, until I realised that although the author had never used the words 'binomial theorem' that was exactly where I was. Yet at Nuffield a young graduate called Graham Pyatt - later a professor of mathematics - coached me in statistics out of sheer kindness until I could handle fairly complex data and perform routine statistical tests, at least with the help of a 'cookbook'.

Among the lectures and seminars I attended at other colleges were Herbert Hart's on punishment, and my contribution to one discussion had a momentous effect on the rest of my life. My sabbatical had made me realise that I would give a lot to exchange bureaucracy for an academic life. Not only had the Scottish Office asked me to master nine different specialisms in 11 years: I was embarrassed by the image of the civil servant presented by the media. It was detectable even in the literature of the day. The only authors in whose novels a civil servant was a respected figure were Iris Murdoch and C.P. Snow. Finally I had realised that I myself lacked something which the good civil servant had: perhaps it was simply pragmatism.

I asked Norman Chester whether he saw any chance of my getting an academic job, but he dismissively said 'None at all'. He hadn't heard of luck. Max Grunhut, the University Reader in

Criminology, was on the point of retirement. A faction led by Chester wanted to abolish his Readership and use its salary to fund another sort of appointment. Peterson, the Oxford educationalist, supported him, publicly declaring the view that criminology was too 'banausic' a subject for Oxford. ('Banausic' means 'blacksmiths' work' - more academic snobbery.) Herbert Hart and Rupert Cross, the famous lawyers, were determined that the post should be filled. Through Hart's wife Jenifer, a fellow of Nuffield, I was asked if I would apply. It meant a drop in salary, but I was so enthusiastic that this seemed a minor consideration.

So I applied. I was interviewed by Hart, Cross, Isaiah Berlin and a now hostile Chester. In an effort to discredit *A Short History* he said that he supposed that had been my thesis. No, I said, my thesis was represented by a short footnote late in the book. I got the job.

9. AN UNDESERVED APPOINTMENT

"A professional fellow in statu pupillari?
(The Proctors)

So in my forties I became a don. Since I knew no academic criminology the man who should have got the job was Terence Morris of the LSE. He and his equally impressive wife Pauline had completed their well-known study of Pentonville Prison, and he already had a reputation for brilliance. Other English criminologists expected him to be chosen, and I still don't know why he wasn't. Oxford's sceptical attitude to sociologists may have had something to do with it, but I still feel guilty about my luck.

Having appointed me the University naturally expected Nuffield to make me a professorial fellow. Chester agreed, but things soon went wrong. He received a letter from the Proctors, drawing his attention to the fact that he had given this honour to an undergraduate. (My Edinburgh PhD did not count.) He was embarrassed, but I was not. There had been little point in 1939 in paying for a degree which was unlikely to be of use to me; and the fees had piled up over a quarter of a century. I saw no reason why I should not remain modestly and frugally *in statu pupillari*; but Chester was very anxious that his college should not be regarded as disreputable, so I let the college pay my fees.

Enough about Chester. There was more stimulating company in the college. Freddie Madden, with whom I had played bad hockey at the House, was a brilliant amateur actor and raconteur. I vividly remember one of his anecdotes. He was in the local orthopaedic hospital, under treatment which involved suspension by means of a collar. In the cubicle opposite a man under leg traction watched him for a time, then said 'Looking at you, guv, reminds me of the job I gotta do next week'. He was a Home

Office hangman, and he entertained Freddie with grisly stories about jobs he had done. Freddie's collar prevented him from protesting, and he could do nothing but swing slowly from south to north and back again.

Also brilliant on the stage was Jean Packman. She modestly described herself as 'too old for Ophelia, too young for Gertrude', but her performance as Kate the Shrew was memorable. The economists were duller, although one later earned a Nobel prize. The most interesting of them was a man who had been struck by lightning while leaning against a wet ruin on Deeside. He remembers a blue flash before falling unconscious. Against the odds, I have also known two other men, both lawyers, who were struck and survived in similar situations. One sustained a burn down his chest and completely fused zippers in his trousers, but no more serious damage; the other's right arm was paralysed for a short time.

A lasting friendship was the result of my successful negotiations to get a sabbatical fellowship for Henry Rollin, the first psychiatrist to publish a book about 'the revolving doors' of the mental hospitals which received petty offenders, treated and discharged them, only to be asked by courts to admit them again within months. He was a bitter critic of the notion of community care for these unfortunates, and would ask 'What community?' It was many years before his scepticism was recognised as justified. He was a great success at Nuffield, and not only because he could be consulted informally about our more eccentric inmates. Many of his friends were musicians, and he drew on them to arrange a series of concerts in college which continued, with his help, long after he had left.

Eccentric inmates we certainly had. Robin Farquharson was a brilliant logician, but suffered from manic episodes. 'Suffered' is the conventional word; but he told me that he enjoyed them. He had been a favoured candidate for an All Souls' fellowship, but forfeited his chances by ringing up the Warden of the college - John Sparrow - in the middle of the night in order to emphasise his genius. During the early stage of a manic episode he was capable of brilliant work, but as the disorder got worse he would disappear, to be found wandering naked in Didcot station. Why Didcot? I think the explanation is simple logistics. The mental hospital in Perth used to receive a higher number of paranoid patients than could be explained, until one of the doctors realised that Perth was as far as a Londoner could get from his pursuers without changing trains. Didcot is where one is apt to find oneself if one leaps onto a train at Oxford without regard to timetables. David Butler was one of the few people who could persuade Robin to come back to college. Being highly intelligent he would forestall any attempt at compulsory 'sectioning' by entering a mental hospital as a voluntary patient, so that he could leave when he pleased. When his research fellowship with us ended he got one at a Cambridge college, which was not, I believe, told of his disorder. Eventually he drifted into the world of urban dossers, and died in a fire in a squat - an example of 'care in the community'.

I have already mentioned the college's collection of 'visiting fellows', most of them selected for their importance in politics, journalism or public affairs. I recall Callaghan striding bravely out of the Common Room to reason with an invasion of student protesters, led by Dummett of All Souls'. I forget what the protest was about: only that there was no violence. I recall being bored by Heath while placed next to him at dinner, when he could talk about nothing but Bangladesh (having just been briefed about it, I imagine, by the Foreign Office). I recall a drunken George Brown groping a woman guest at dessert. Visiting fellows would give seminars, at which it was expressly promised that what they said would not find its way to the news media. Robert Mark could have talked interestingly about his frustrated efforts to purge the Metropolitan Police of corruption, but preferred the duller subject of policing by consent.

It was fortunate that the conditions of my sabbatical leave had required me to stay in the civil service until 1961. I spent my final year trying to civilise the Scottish approved schools, and persuaded them to abandon corporal punishment for girls, but failed to persuade them that staff should share at least one meal a day with inmates. The year's delay gave me a breathing-space in which to learn some academic criminology.

I must first explain that some people are called 'criminologists', especially in the USA, because they have been trained in what we in Britain would call 'the forensic sciences': the distinguishing, for example, of types of blood, hair, dust or other physical evidence that may lead to the identification or conviction of criminals - what was once called 'criminalistics'. 'Profiling' falls into this category. Even in Britain, however, there was a magazine called *The Criminologist*, whose contents were usually sensational rather than professional. Again, books about notorious murderers or rapists are seldom by genuine criminologists, although they can sometimes give police or prosecutors instructive examples of mistakes in detection or the handling of evidence.

The leading English criminologists in the fifties were a trio of emigres from central Europe, Mannheim, Grunhut and Radzinowicz. Mannheim had been the most influential, generating empirical research, writing an authoritative book (*Comparative Criminology*), and fostering several research students who were to make their names, notably Terence Morris and Leslie Wilkins. By the nineteen-sixties, however, he had become paranoid and unapproachable. Grunhut, a judge from Bonn, had written *Penal Reform*, and had been given a room and eventually a University Readership at All Souls; but he was a sick man, and died soon after

I replaced him.

In Cambridge a Pole called Leon Radzinowicz had published the first three volumes of his gigantic *History of English Criminal Law and its Administration*, and had succeeded - in competition with London University - in setting up the first British Institute of Criminology. In it Derrick McLintock was producing a series of statistical studies of sexual crimes and violence, based on police records. In the nineteen-sixties the Institute's interests broadened. Donald West launched his study of the careers of a cohort of London schoolboys, on which he - and later David Farrington - based many publications. Many of the boys are now grandfathers, and their descendants have begun to figure in the study. David Thomas was establishing himself as an authority on sentencing statutes and case-law. Roger Hood was writing about the development of Borstals in England. Richard Sparks and his small team were laying the foundations of the first victim survey to be carried out in Britain, which emphasised the extent to which the Metropolitan Police's records understated reality. In London Trevor Gibbens was developing forensic psychiatry at the Maudsley Hospital.

Fortunately by 1960 the literature was not as vast as now. Quite a lot of it was of little more than historical interest. Lombroso had been discredited, chiefly by a painstaking prison doctor in England, but was still revered in Italy and Harvard, where Ernest Hootton had published volumes on his inconclusive measurements of convicts' crania. It was he who solemnly discovered that many murderers were widowers. Harvard's Sheldon had spawned ectomorphs, endomorphs and mesomorphs, which would have pleased Lombroso; but more lasting were the contributions of the American sociologists, notably the 'Chicago school', who focused attention on cultures and sub-cultures.

By way of contrast English criminology was largely the work

of psychoanalysts, psychiatrists and psychologists. Psychiatrists, notably Norwood East and Trevor Gibbens, had made important contributions, for example on paedophilia. The psychoanalytic contributions were less impressive. Glover, prompted by an observation of Freud's, had declared that unconscious guilt was the key to the problem of delinquency: Freud had the sense to explain only *some* delinquencies in this way. Bowlby, the populariser of maternal deprivation, had studied 44 juvenile thieves, with psychoanalytic conclusions. Psychologists, notably Gordon Trasler, were applying learning theory to the explanation of more normal delinquency. Barbara Wootton, however, had just published *Social Science and Social Pathology*, which laid waste most empirical searches for explanations of crime, as well as most social workers' beliefs, and most of what had been written about psychopaths. Originally an economist, later a magistrate, she was one of those intellectual helicopters who hover over other academics' fields, spraying defoliants. In person she was aggressive but stimulating, and I persuaded her to give several seminars at Nuffield, and served on one of her committees.

English sociologists were taking their cues from America, and spent a great deal of energy in trying to discredit psychology, perhaps because, as Philip Burgess once put it, one of the jobs of psychologists is to follow the cavalry of sociology with the shovel of empirical research. I had not realised how much antagonism there was between the two disciplines, and early in my time at Oxford made the mistake of inviting the Halseys to meet the Argyles for dinner at our home. Halsey, an LSE sociologist, attacked Michael Argyle the social psychologist with a venom I have seldom seen equalled, even on television, and never at a dinner-table. Halsey had trained as a fighter pilot, but too late to allow him to shoot anyone down, although his car-driving was spectacular. He was Director of Barnett House, the training institution for social workers, but did more, as a fellow at Nuffield, to develop academic sociology in Oxford than anyone else of his generation. He was also, however, a man with a strong social conscience, as he goes to great lengths to make clear in his autobiography, which would have been more interesting if it had explained some of his many animosities.

His absent-mindedness meant many wasted hours for the pupils who turned up for tutorials, but once involved me in a fascinating encounter. He had invited R.D. Laing (*The Divided Self*) to dine in college before addressing an academic audience. An embarrassed butler whispered to me over sherry that a Dr Laing had turned up but not Mr Halsey. I made up an excuse for Halsey and looked after Laing. He seemed an ordinary, respectably dressed Glaswegian, whose books I had read, but at dinner he was silent and ill at ease. It was with relief that I escorted him into Oxford to his meeting. As soon as we neared the hall he took off his tie, ruffled his hair, hung a lit cigarette from his mouth and transformed himself into the slightly farouche celebrity which he knew his audience expected. By this time Halsey had remembered to turn up, and I went home.

My next encounter with Laing was at Yale, when I was spending a short sabbatical teaching in the Law School. He gave a seminar to the staff in which he argued that one should never interfere with someone who had decided on suicide. He was unmoved by the distress which suicides inflict on others, and brushed aside the point that suicidal depressions can be successfully treated. But his most harmful contribution to psychiatry was the theory - borrowed from an American - that most schizophrenias are the effects of 'double messages' from parents. It caused countless parents to blame themselves unjustly. His subsequent theorising grew wilder and wilder, and led him to follow strange gurus, but stopped him doing more harm. It was said that on his death-bed 'his last words were that he did not want a doctor to be called'. He would have been insulted by this bowdlerisation. What he really said was 'Doctor? What fucking doctor?'

My own dinner-guests were usually psychologists, sociologists or psychiatrists who had performed at one of my seminars. One of them was Richard Hunter, who had just published the historic revelation that George III's madness was really porphyria. (His mother, Ida McAlpine, had unearthed the evidence in medical archives.) Guests were usually treated with respect, but after dinner another guest came up to us and said 'Are you the man who published all that nonsense about George III?' I think he was trying to start a conversation, but if so he failed.

Swotting up criminology was one thing; teaching it was more formidable. Most of my students were graduates, and I was conscious of my inexperience. Once again I was in the grip of fear. I envied Halsey, who could enter the seminar room a minute or so late and begin 'On the way here I wondered whether to talk to you about the history of the subject or about the present state of play'. My own first lectures were based almost verbatim on laborious notes, and my delivery must have been intolerably tedious. The army had forced me to be audible at a distance, and the civil service had taught me how to steer a plausible line between precision and vagueness. My notes looked better when turned into a text-book: at that time there wasn't a British one.

Another of my shortcomings, however, was that I had never dealt face to face with criminals. I could not begin a lecture like Walter Sprott, the psychologist. 'My friend the burglar says ...' always produced a titillated flutter. Acquaintance with criminals had snob value. I was not alone, of course. In those days one could take a university qualification in criminology without actually talking to a criminal, as I was to find at Cambridge. I had visited Scottish prisons, and talked to prisoners, but only on the sort of visits that one pays to a zoo. So it was my good luck to be asked by Bill

Gray, the first medical superintendent of the newly opened psychiatric prison at Grendon, to help launch a group counselling programme. My initiation began with discussions with the prison officers who were to be group leaders, as I was; and at first one of the officers helped me with my group of prisoners, until I learned the argot. At that time discussions focused on staff-prisoner and prisoner-prisoner relations, not on the prisoners' offences. This was one of the mistakes of the therapeutic techniques of the post-war decades. It took prison psychologists and probation officers far too long to see the need for offenders to be forced to face both the motivation and the consequences of what they had done. So group counselling's only beneficial effect was the improvement of relations within prisons and borstals.

For me, however, it was an education in prisoners' ways of thinking. Eventually I was allowed to bring one or two graduate students - usually aspiring social workers - to meetings, and they learned so much that one of them asked why they couldn't have similar meetings with mentally normal prisoners. This took some contriving, but the Governor of Oxford Prison, John Brophy, was so near retirement that he was prepared to take the risk. At first two officers had to be present, and no women were accepted; but the officers soon got bored, and it was not long before they were replaced by women students from Barnett House. The students had to commit themselves to attend four consecutive weekly meetings. The prisoners did not have to commit themselves, but most of them stayed as long as they could. We made it clear that we were not using them for research, nor trying to reform them, but hoping to learn from them about prison life and the criminal process.

We certainly did. They became remarkably frank about their delinquencies, both 'inside' and outside. Some were boastful. Safe-blowing carried prestige, and one man claimed to have unlocked a safe which had a special new kind of lock. 'Not as new as all that' said another, to which all he could reply was 'Well it was the first we'd come across in High Wycombe'. They often strayed from the point, but did not mind being dragged back; and their behaviour was so good that I never had to use the alarm bell. I looked for it once, when a young undergraduate lawyer, during a discussion of their sentences, burst out 'You're all guilty as hell and deserved far more than you got'; but the prisoners just laughed at him. I was embarrassed rather than alarmed by the behaviour of a magistrate who tried to sort out their private lives, as if she were an agony aunt, but they seemed to expect nothing better from a magistrate. The classes were of special interest to visitors from many other countries, who were astonished at the frankness of the discussions.

A lurking danger was the attempts of one or two prisoners to set up a correspondence with female students (who were warned never to give an address), but only one woman was inveigled into this, and as she was not a student but an experienced colleague I did not feel responsible for the mild pestering she suffered. My own experience of persecution was at the hands of a knife-carrying Scot who had been in my Grendon group after stabbing a policeman, and whose craving for drink would bring him to call on me at college, where he once vomited on Jean Floud's doorstep before reaching my room. I would never allow him more than one dram, but was very scared when he once took out his sheath-knife. 'Ha' he said 'that frightened you', and put it away again. He had been under treatment at the Littlemore Hospital for alcoholism, but it refused to readmit him without a recommendation from the probation service, who would not give him one. Unthinkingly I remarked that they would have if he'd committed an offence, whereupon he went out, grabbed a radio from a shop and tried to sell it to another shop, which duly called the police. With bad grace the probation service at last found him a place at the Littlemore, and I lost touch with him, without great regret.

More interesting was the middle-aged man who consulted me out of the blue one day. By now I had learned not to have these unsolicited visitors shown to my room, so I walked him round the college's mini-canal. His story was a strange one, as Dr Watson would have said. He had consulted a series of orthopaedic specialists about agonising neck-pain, until one of them spotted and dealt with the cause. He complained to one of his previous consultants about his failure to detect the obvious, and when he received no apology threw a brick through his window. The police let him off with a caution, but ever since, he said, they had kept him under constant observation. Could I get them to stop? I asked him how disturbing he found this, and his reply was interesting. He resented it, but found it reassuring because he knew they would intervene next time he tried to do something violent. All I could do was tell him he was lucky - which I think he accepted - and usher him out of the college. As he left he said 'They'll be waiting for me outside', and in a way they were, because the Crown Court was sitting that day opposite the college, and a policeman was idling opposite the college lodge.

More worrying was the ex-patient from Broadmoor who called on me, as a result of one of my radio broadcasts. He had been detained there after trying to strangle an 11-year-old boy with whom he had been in love, in order to prevent him from entering puberty. Much later he had seemed fit for release under supervision, which lasted for several years until his probation officer was posted elsewhere. He had then drifted to London, and found a job in a youth club, of all places. He was still attracted to boys, but claimed that he would never again be so silly. He talked so interestingly and freely that with his consent I invited some of my trainee social workers from Barnett House to meet him. All but one said that they had benefitted. The exception was a puritanical Scot who accused me of exploiting the man. Another Scot later accused me of exploiting my prisoners in the same way. I argued that they were no more being exploited than a patient in a hospital who agrees to be examined by medical students. To do my critics justice I suspect that what disturbed them was that unlike hospital patients my 'subjects' were naively exposing more of themselves than they realised, in a way which should take place only in a confessional. Yet I saw no sign that they were disturbed by the experience.

Another broadcast of mine produced a postcard, signed 'Dewsnip', from a man in Newcastle who threatened violence for an undisclosed reason. As Newcastle was fairly distant I didn't worry; but it was followed a week or two later by another postcard, saying that he was coming to get me, and postmarked in a village in Staffordshire. I was in some suspense, and reminded the college porters not to direct unrecognised visitors to my room. No more postcards arrived, nor did he. I was to encounter a more persistent persecutor in Cambridge.

None of this, however, was academically respectable. The Home Office were as anxious as the Law Faculty that criminological research should continue to be done at Oxford, and were very ready to fund anything sensible. I knew quite a lot about psychiatry, and one of the research assistants whom I inherited from Grunhut was Sarah McCabe, who had done the fieldwork for their study of offenders put on probation and under psychiatric treatment. The Mental Health Act 1959 had just overhauled the system for sentencing mentally disordered offenders. So we launched a follow-up of a whole year's cohort of offenders committed to psychiatric treatment as in-patients. At one stage it seemed likely that psychiatric consultants would refuse to help with our dossiers because neither of us was medically qualified; but Sarah's brother, Pat McGrath (father of the novelist) was Medical Superintendent of Broadmoor, and persuaded the BMA to bless the project. In the event very few psychiatrists were uncooperative. One was an Irish doctor in Broadmoor, who thus deprived us of some important female cases, I am not sure whether from principle or laziness. Even so we managed to follow up more than 1200 adults for two years and more.

All this took years to organise, added to which was the two-year follow-up and the analysis of data, again with the help of Harwell's computers.. The burden of handling the data fell on Sarah McCabe. Meanwhile I had realised how little was known about the pre-history of the subject. One well-known book had even said that the insanity defence was not accepted before 1800. I soon found that this was wrong by about seven centuries. Another delusion was that the popularity of the defence had increased after Hadfield's acquittal of trying to murder George III, and again after M'Naghten's murder of Peel's secretary. My statistical study of the Old Bailey Sessions Papers showed that this was not so. Again, there was a strange Act of Henry VIII which nobody had explained, laying down that insanity did not bar execution if the crime was treason. Elton, the Tudor historian, did not answer my letter about it; but my excellent research assistant, Norma Wright, suggested a search in Henry's State Papers. She found a copy of a letter from the Spanish ambassador, telling his master that Lady Rocheford, condemned to death for being an accomplice in the Queen's adultery, had feigned madness to save her life. This was firm evidence that the rule against executing offenders who went mad after being found guilty was at least as old as the 16th century, so that Henry had to pass his Act in order to execute her (Elizabeth repealed it). The origins of diminished responsibility, too, were obscure, and even Scottish lawyers had written questionable stuff about them. So I wrote *Crime and Insanity in England,* vol.1 while waiting for the data about our follow-up. It was the main reason for the award of a D.Litt by Oxford. This was also the first higher doctorate awarded to a Nuffield fellow by the university, and I had expected that it would at last make me respectable in Chester's eyes; but he never mentioned it.

It would have been difficult to follow up our cohort of offender-patients without a small research unit, and with the help of a grant from the Nuffield Foundation we persuaded the University to create one. The Law Faculty were far from enthusiastic about this free gift, but with the support of Rupert Cross, by now the Vinerian Professor of Law, we were allotted two rooms in the new Bodleian Library. (Years later I was intrigued to learn that Radzinowicz' renowned Institute began as an office in the Cambridge University Library, surrounded by the same lack of enthusiasm.) The task of managing our small Penal Research Unit, with its staff of two, fell on Sarah McCabe, who handled it admirably, while I burrowed in libraries or worked on committees. When Roger Hood succeeded me the Unit became The Oxford Centre for Criminology, and achieved a more dignified address.

It must have been in the early sixties that Charles Cunningham, by now the Permanent Undersecretary of State at the Home Office, tried to persuade me to return to the civil service as the head of his research department. I liked him, but had dire recollections of working directly under him, and had after all gone through a lot in order to escape from the civil service. Charles was rather put out when I refused without the usual polite gesture of asking for time to consider his offer. Nevertheless I soon found myself spending about one day a week commuting to meetings in London, having a breakfast game of chess on the train with Rupert Cross. Blind from infancy, he had played well enough in his youth to be a competitor in national tournaments, and he did not even need a blind man's board to beat me. I have seen him leave the game in a complex state for dinner at All Souls', drink enough to floor me, and return to win the game. His friendship is one of my pleasantest

106

memories of Oxford.

The breakfast rail journey to London was straightforward. Coming back one often had to change at Didcot or be carried on to Swindon. One day this befell both me and the Oxfordshire Director of Social Work, the well-known Barbara Kahan. There seemed to be no way of retracing our steps by rail, so I suggested hitch-hiking, which she had never done. We were duly picked up by a kindly lorry-driver. At journey's end Barbara startled him by saying 'Thank you so much. Now I know how my girls get pregnant'.

A sabbatical term at Berkeley was my first experience of the United States. Berkeley itself was a drab town, but a policeman in my class took me on one of his eight-hour patrols in Oakland, which was exciting enough. We broke down a hotel door to extract a week-old corpse. Next we were called to help another cop arrest a large black who was beating the cop's head on the pavement when we reached the scene. By the time we all reached the police station it had received half-a-dozen telephone calls about the brutality of the arrest. When we were called to a suspected burglary at a laundry I was nearly shot because I had not taken seriously the order to stay in the police-car, and stupidly peered inside the building. Later we had the usual free meal in a diner where the owner valued the regular visits of a cop.

Towards the end of my time at Oxford my wife and I were shocked by the trial of my Scottish Office colleague, George Pottinger, for his involvement in the Poulson scandal. George, a brilliant administrator, had by this time become head of the Department of Agriculture, and was spoken of as likely to succeed the Permanent Head of the whole Scottish Office. Poulson was an architect and building contractor who competed for large development schemes, including the Aviemore tourist centre. He had struck up a friendship with Pottinger, at that time an Under-Secretary on a special assignment to stimulate business interest in such enterprises. The friendship led to Pottinger's receiving lavish gifts from Poulson - holidays in Switzerland, a car and even a custom-built house beside Pottinger's golf-club at Muirfield. It was at the Muirfield clubhouse, in the middle of a black-tie dinner, that Pottinger was finally arrested, which seemed to me a sadistic feature of the proceedings.

He was tried at Leeds on charges of corruption. Later he maintained that he was tried in England because no Scottish court would have convicted him. His defence was that while he had now and then advised Poulson on the drafting of letters to the Scottish Office he had never used his position there to influence any decision in Poulson's favour: a claim that was never really disproved. It certainly seemed that he had failed to tell his Department of the gifts he was receiving from Poulson, but that was merely a breach of Estacode, the official code of conduct for civil servants, and the explanation may have been merely that he knew he would have been disciplined for accepting them. His case was complicated by a loyal secretary who destroyed at least one relevant letter.

The head of the Scottish Office, at that time Haddow the golfer, encouraged George to be optimistic about the result of the Fraud Squad's investigation, but gave rather equivocal evidence in court, for which George never forgave him. In this and other ways the trial went badly. Asked in the witness-box about his relationship with Poulson he let slip the remark that 'he was not quite one of us' - a phrase which later found its way into *Yes, Prime Minister*. It so happened that I was a member of a Whitehall committee which included the trial judge, who confirmed that this remark, though irrelevant, went down badly with him and almost certainly with the jury. In St Andrew's House there were quite a few colleagues who thought - as I did - that he deserved condemnation for disgracing the civil service, but some of whom doubted whether he had done anything to deserve a criminal conviction. One very senior man felt so strongly that he bequeathed a cassette on the subject to the National Library of Scotland.

George was sentenced to five years' imprisonment, a severe sentence reduced to four by the Court of Criminal Appeal. In those days a prisoner became eligible for parole after a third of his sentence. George persuaded some of his eminent friends and acquaintances - including Home - to write to the Home Office on his behalf, oddly unaware that this too would not count in his favour. It should not have counted against him either, of course, and when I was a member of the Parole Board a 'first-timer' such as he would have been released as soon as eligible. For some reason he was not, perhaps because he had accepted so many gifts over a long period; but at that time the Board did not give its reasons for adverse decisions.

George's was not the only kind of case in which I disagreed with the Parole Board's policies, and while I was a member of it I was not popular with its chairman Lord Windlesham or his successor, Lord Colville. For example the Board felt obliged to refuse parole to drug couriers from abroad, mostly desperate women from Nigeria and South America, because on release they would be deported and could not be under the post-release supervision which was in theory part of their sentence. This struck me as an artificial reason for discriminating against them, especially since the Act expressly envisaged the possibility of parole without supervision. I argued this, but theory prevailed and they served the whole of their sentences, unlike home-grown couriers.

Again, the Board did not favour paroling offenders who refused to admit their guilt, as men convicted of sexual or violent offences sometimes did. In the Board's eyes this was a failure to respond adequately to their sentence. Although not involved in any such cases I was troubled, because the reality is more complex. Some prisoners don't want to admit their guilt, especially when it involves child-molesting, because of the likely reactions of staff and fellow prisoners. Some believe that their violence was justified by self-defence or provocation. Some may actually be innocent. In 1977 a man called Robert Brown was jailed for life for murder. In 1988 he was refused parole because he maintained his innocence (to do the Parole Board justice he had signed a confession while in police custody). In 1999 the High Court told the Parole Board that it must not reason in this way, but it was not until late in 2002 that the Court of Appeal decided that Brown's conviction was unsafe (and probably mistaken) because the senior detective in his case was 'deeply corrupt'. Later I'll discuss other awkwardnesses created by innocence.

To return to George Pottinger: he and his wife came to live near Cambridge, and we would occasionally meet. He had spent most of his sentence at Ford, the prison for the middle-aged and middle-class (one of the prisoners in my seminars at Bedford Prison complained that most of the recreational tables in the evenings were taken up by bankers' bridge-fours). George, who wrote with style, completed a novel there. Some of the novel's action took place in Italy. Like all private compositions in prison it had to be vetted before he could take it out with him, and the vetting was done - with George's consent - by the governor's wife, who read novels. Her verdict was *nihil obstat,* but with the rider that there was dialogue here and there in Italian, which would not do, since French was the only foreign language acceptable in a novel. George explained that since the dialogue was between Italians that would not do either; but he was obliged to translate the dialogue into French. After release he published several books, but not novels. He remained a member of the Savile Club, although forced to resign from the New Club in Edinburgh. He had always been a remarkably good tennis player, and collapsed on the court during a foursome at the age of 82 - a fairly kind death.

But that was some years after I left Oxford. My farewell was celebrated by a dinner party at All Souls', given by my friend Rupert Cross. It was honoured by the presence of the then Warden, John Sparrow. He has since been the victim of an authorised biography by John Lowe which emphasises his undeniable failings, among them a dislike of women; but my wife, who sat beside him, remembers him as one of the most entertaining and considerate dons she had conversed with. The picture his biographer paints is of a man with all the attributes of a scholar except the dedication. He wanted the Wardenship more than anything else - and wrote some odd letters in his efforts to get it - because for him All Souls was the best of clubs. Like most clubmen he did not want changes; and against all sorts of pressures he managed to preserve something very like the *status quo* until he retired. Tragically he then went through an alcoholic phase, in which he behaved so badly that the college forbade him to dine in hall.

It was sad that after leaving Oxford I saw so little of Rupert Cross, who had done so much to smooth my path at Oxford, and had become a close friend. He was gradually succumbing to cancer, but made so light of it that I did not realise how close to death he was, and came back from abroad to hear that he had died.

10. THOSE COMMITTEES

"Exactly what is mens rea?"

(Lord Butler)

A whole book could be written about the committees which have agonised over crime or punishment, but it would be tedious. I shall chronicle only a few with which I have been concerned.

In the early sixties the Labour opposition began to make a political issue out of crime, and talked of the need for a comprehensive review of the situation and the issues involved. An insecure government felt obliged to trump the opposition by appointing a Royal Commission on the Penal System. Leon Radzinowicz, who had expressed grave - and justified - doubts about the notion of a general review, was not consulted. Cunningham, by now the permanent head of the Home Office, was far from enthusiastic. Brooke the Home Secretary, however, persuaded the Cabinet and the Prime Minister (by that time Home) that it was politically necessary. The Royal Commission were given what Radzinowicz called a 'suicidal remit', of enormous scope, with a chairman (Lord Amory) whose unfitness soon became apparent. Radzinowicz himself had felt obliged, in spite of his doubts, to accept the invitation to be a member, but soon began to discuss with other members - Barbara Wootton and the Bishop of Exeter for example - whether the Commission had any hope of achieving its purpose. My own experience of appearing before them as a 'witness' was bizarre. As soon as I began to give my views on the proper aims of sentencing, which is what they had asked me to do, they began to argue with each other, unchecked by the Chairman and uninterrupted by me. Eventually, in 1967, nearly half the members resigned, and the Prime Minister (by now Harold Wilson) advised the Queen to dissolve the Commission. It was an episode without precedent in the history of Royal Commissions.

It had an interesting echo 30 years on. *The Times* published a letter signed by my friend Louis Blom-Cooper (the well-known QC and former Chairman of the Howard League), by Lord Allen of Abbeydale (a former permanent head of the Home Office) and by at least two eminent judges, solemnly proposing the setting up of a Royal Commission on Crime and Punishment. If the idea had been naive in 1964 it was doubly naive at the end of the century, and I said so in another letter to *The Times*. Such a Commission had as much hope of getting anywhere as a Commission on Disease and its Treatment. Strangely, Radzinowicz's last book reproved me for calling the proposal 'naive'.

Meanwhile, however, the Home Secretary had tried another expedient - a standing Advisory Council on the Penal System, expected to produce recommendations on sensibly defined problems referred to it by the Home Office. In due course I became a member. Its reports were constructive and thorough - I am tempted to say 'too thorough'. They were usually the work of subcommittees, whose chairmen, chosen by the Council chairman, Sir Kenneth Younger the Labour politician, wanted to make their names with a thick report. The result was an enormous amount of homework for the secretariat, and a report which was often too controversial for the times and far too late to wait for. Younger himself oversaw the work which led to the report on the custodial treatment of young adult offenders. The secretary at the time was Sidney Norris, a product of the Cambridge Institute who believed in the possibilities of reforming character, and he and Younger arranged a tour of American institutions which inspired the committee with what is called 'therapeutic optimism'. One minor symptom of this particular form of delusion was that the committee refused to recommend that courts should be allowed to suspend custodial sentences for young adults (as they could for adults), because that would deprive the young of the benefits of a therapeutic regime. Lady James and I, being more realistic about the effects of such institutions, recorded strong dissent. I cite this as an example of an injustice inspired by unreal hopes and travellers' tales. Twenty years later it has not been remedied.

Yet some of the committees were worthwhile. Barbara Wootton's was an example, and was responsible for the innovation called 'community service', which now seems to be effective slightly more often than probation in preventing, or at least postponing, recidivism. Barbara Wootton was a chairwoman who could be peremptory without giving offence.

An important member in the early days was Bishop Mortimer of Exeter, who had been one of the wreckers of the Royal Commission. He chaired the report on detention centres, which successfully recommended that they no longer be used for girls. Unfortunately this particular bishopric had for long been associated in my mind with Sydney Smith. When a lady asked the Smith of Smiths whether he believed in the apostolic succession his reply was 'Madam, I am compelled to, by the direct descent of the Bishop of Exeter from Judas Iscariot'. I mentioned this by way of small talk at lunch once in college, whereupon the man whom I was trying to entertain said 'Bishop Mortimer's my uncle'. He didn't seem to be mollified when I hastened to explain that Sydney Smith was talking about a long-dead incumbent of the see.

I myself had briefly chaired a council in the sixties. Because I had been involved with probation in Scotland, where we nearly succeeded in combining umpteen local departments into a national service, the Home Office thought that I was really enthusiastic, and made me a member and later chairman of the Advisory Council on Probation and After-Care. In practice ACPAC wasn't allowed to give much advice, merely to comment on ready-made proposals from the Home Office, and when I was asked by a new minister whether it was doing a useful job I said 'No', and was glad to administer the quietus. No tears were shed by anyone at ACPAC's funeral. I chaired one or two other committees, but their reports - on social workers' legal training and on violence in Scotland - were too predictable to be interesting.

The most interesting committee for me was Lord Butler's, on mentally abnormal offenders, which had nothing to do with the Advisory Council. Watching Butler manage it was itself instructive. He knew nothing about psychiatry, and not much more about criminal law. He never quite understood what *mens rea* meant, and instead of asking one of the lawyers on the committee he would ring me up secretly at home in the evening to ask me to explain it again. Cunningly, he split his huge committee into two halves, each under a judge. One would sort out the law, the other all the non-legal problems. He attended only the full meetings, at which the subcommittees would present tidy proposals on paper. Even when they led to fierce and unresolved disagreements Butler would put an end to the argument by saying 'Well that seems to be agreed. Let's go on to the next item ...' The unfortunate secretary had to record an agreement of sorts, but his record was seldom challenged. It was crude, but it worked. Unusually, the membership included a journalist, Ronald Butt, and since civil servants distrust such people I wondered whether this was Butler's idea. However that may be I can recall no ill-advised leaks during our long and agonised deliberations. And to do Butler justice it was he whose speeches in the Lords shamed the government into financing the new semi-secure hospitals which his report had recommended.

Among the committee's instructive visits was one to C Wing of Parkhurst, a special unit for violent men with personality disorders. A doctor and I were also allowed to have a short talk, in his cell, with the notorious Graham Young, who had poisoned so many of his relatives and workmates, not out of animosity but out of sheer interest in pharmacology. In Parkhurst his fellow prisoners refused to eat at the same table. Wisely, perhaps, for after Young had been observed feeding bread to the goldfish in the pond of the exercise yard they all turned belly-up. He had ground match-heads into the bread. Dr Douglas Acres and I had a short talk with him, most of it about the work he was given to do. He was as reserved as I would have been in the circumstances, but as we left his cell Dr Acres said 'A marked lack of affect there, don't you think?' I nearly asked him what sort of affect he expected an intelligent lifer to display when two unexpected strangers dropped in to chat.

Another person who chaired committees superbly was Jean Floud, formerly a Fellow of Nuffield but by now Principal of Newnham at Cambridge. Louis Blom-Cooper, as Chairman of the Howard League, had managed to get a grant from America to fund a working party on the subject of dangerous offenders. It was a time of conflict between civil libertarians who thought it immoral to detain people to prevent them from doing what they might not do, and 'social defenders' who considered that the need to protect the public was paramount. Louis wanted me to chair it, but I knew that my own views were too strong and suggested Jean, with a doctoral student from my Institute, Warren Young, to act as secretary. Both proved excellent choices. Jean Floud's intelligence and humour prevented the usual schisms from destroying the committee, and unlike most chairpersons she drafted a subtle and thorough report, which was commercially published as *Dangerousness and Criminal Justice*. Unfortunately it was too complex for most readers. I even heard Lord Allen of Abbeydale, the former head of the Home Office, discuss it at a seminar in terms which made it clear that he hadn't read much of it. It was another example of a publication which was too thorough to be influential.

The environments in which committees sit can vary greatly. The Floud Working Party - when not visiting 'lifer' prisons - met in the agreeable Principal's House of Newnham College, in a room which looked out on a famous garden. The Hodgson Committee, by way of contrast, met after working hours in a smoke-filled room off Holborn. Like the Floud Committee it was the creation of the Howard League, but concerned with the more esoteric problems of compensating victims of crime and depriving criminals of their gains. Sir Derek Hodgson, a well-known judge, chaired it with patience, but could not avoid such conflict with the Secretary, Andrew Nicol, over some technicalities that the latter drafted a note of dissent. A more vivid recollection for me, however, was the extraordinary sensitivity of a Deputy Assistant Commissioner from the Metropolitan Police. I had produced some evidence that not all *provincial* police forces complied with the policy of giving victims of crime a leaflet about their right to claim compensation. The Deputy Assistant Commissioner somehow took this as a reflection on the Met, and his attack on me was so abusive that he had to be gently admonished by Hodgson, after which he absented himself. The report was published commercially as *The Profits of Crime*, and unlike the Floud Report contributed several ideas to later legislation.

The Bridge Working Party on Judicial Studies and Information was really about the training of judges, and in the consultative paper which we issued we made the mistake of saying so. The word 'training' so affronted the judges that we had to ban it from our final report, and talk about 'judicial studies'. I was the only non-lawyer on the committee, apart from the representatives of the Home Office and Lord Chancellor's Office. It opened my eyes to the fact that QCs, some with no experience of criminal work, were being appointed to preside over difficult trials, and to choose between a complex variety of sentences, with only a weekend's training in miserably spartan quarters at Roehampton. At the first meeting Sir Nigel Bridge (as he then was) asked what theories of punishment were, and I had to explain, as if to first-year undergraduates, that some people believed that the main aim of punishment was retribution, while others thought that it was deterrence, and yet others that it was the assertion of a society's values. The news seemed to worry the working-party. This emphasised how few lawyers had studied jurisprudence; but to be fair remarkably few courses of jurisprudence dealt with theories of punishment in those days.

I felt very conscious, however, that at my Institute was a man who knew far more about the legal technicalities of sentencing than I did, and persuaded Bridge to co-opt David Thomas, who eventually became responsible for most of the training and information documents on sentencing for judges. Most of our recommendations for ensuring that new judges were better prepared were implemented, but one important one was not. We proposed that the organisation for providing courses and information should be based in a university, where it would have access to well-supplied libraries and other facilities. The Lord Chancellor's Office and the senior judges were too afraid that this would subvert judicial independence, and the idea was rejected, ostensibly on the ground of cost.

Throughout my time as chairman or member of these councils, committees and working parties - which was probably what earned me my CBE - I kept on recalling what it was like to be a committee secretary, as I had so often been when I was a young civil servant. The meetings themselves are only the tip of an iceberg of paperwork, most of it submerged for ever. Writing minutes that will satisfy the egoists is the least part of it. Some committees hunger for statistics, some for hasty research, and they all want an excuse for visits to other countries. I was not surprised when the Home Office became disillusioned about the value of them, and preferred 'working-parties' chaired by senior civil servants.

11. CAMBRIDGE

"Does one leave before the Vice-Chancellor?"
(A Vice-Chancellor's wife)

In 1972 Cambridge set about finding a replacement for Sir Leon Radzinowicz, the Director of the well-known Institute which he had founded with the help of money from Wolfson and encouragement from Butler at the Home Office. I was not sure who the other short-listed candidates would be, but I was later told that one of them was Leslie Wilkins, who deserves more than a mention.

Like me he had entered university life after a series of non-academic jobs, but after overcoming far more serious obstacles. The son of a shopkeeper and a deeply religious mother, he went from school to a clerical post in the Ministry of Labour, where he spent the early years of war. A gift for statistics took him into research and administration in the RAF, where he incurred reprimands from superior officers for endangering pilots' morale. He had been questioning them about defects in the designs of their aircraft - the first example of his originality. He left the RAF for a post in the Social Survey, where his merits were appreciated. From there he was transferred to the Home Office's Research Unit, where - in collaboration with Herman Mannheim - he produced his famous *Prediction Methods in Relation to Borstal Training* - Actuarial attempts to predict individuals' success or failure were not entirely new, but this book was responsible for the hundreds of penological studies which emulated it. Its heyday is now past because the major predictors of recidivism have long since been established: gender, age, type of offence and of course previous similar delinquency. As an American psychologist once said 'Nothing predicts behaviour like behaviour'. Research unearths new predictors, but they don't improve precision by much, and are alternatives to each other rather than indispensable. Nevertheless this was probably the most important development in penology in the last half-century, because it not only corrected the 'clinical' assessments of offenders by probation officers and psychiatrists - especially in cases said to be 'dangerous' - but also made possible realistic comparisons of the effectiveness of different treatments.

Wilkins, however, ran true to form, and incurred the wrath of the Home Office by publishing a letter in *The Times* which implied that not everyone in the department agreed with the Home Secretary's drug-abuse policy. He resigned, to become a Reader in Glasgow University. Being made to feel unwanted there he got a United Nations post in Japan, and then a professorship in the Berkeley School of Criminology. His originality again provoked resentment when his graduate students saw his first examination paper for his course in research methods:

"Write five examination-type questions relating to the content of the course. Answer three."

One can see the merit of this device, but also the reason for his students' outrage. It required them to think like examiners, in a way that might be called 'meta-examination', a word Leslie would have liked.

On the death of the Dean of the School, ex-Sheriff Lohman, Wilkins became Acting Dean. Unfortunately this was a time of conflict between students and administrators, and Wilkins, lacking Lohman's political skill and connections, found himself again at odds with his bosses. His reputation for research, however, soon found him a professorship at the new university at Albany, New York State, in extraordinary buildings originally designed for Teheran. Some years later, when he applied for the Chair and Directorship at Cambridge, he rather naively proposed that he should combine this position with his better-paid professorship at Albany. Retirement more or less ended his career, but he spent most of his remaining years as Editor of the *Howard Journal* in Cambridge, where he died at the age of 85, a social scientist whose originality deserved more credit.

He may have got the impression that he could combine two major appointments from Radzinowicz's own life-style, which involved the delegation of almost all his teaching and administration. In 1970 he had tried to persuade me to be his Deputy Director by quite improperly promising me his Directorship and Chair as the ultimate reward; but I had learned by then to sup with a long spoon at his table. A few years later I applied for his chair in the normal way, and got it. I didn't want the Directorship as well, but was told that the university couldn't afford to fill it with someone else. It was not until 1998 that my successor persuaded them that they could afford it.

Leon Radzinowicz was a hard act to follow. A stocky, blue-chinned man who never lost his Danziger accent, he had achieved his position by industry and charm. His charm was exercised - in at least four languages - on everyone with whom he had to deal, except his own staff. When I succeeded him it was some time before I could exorcise their insecurities. I can think of only one staff member - Roger Hood - who became and remained a loyal friend of his until his death, at the age of 93, in Philadelphia. Conversation with him, although entertaining, was always about criminology or criminologists, and my impression was that he had no other interests and no recreations. Even so, the criminological scene would have been duller without him.

The most visible products of his industry were the five volumes of his *History of English Criminal Law and its Administration*, which dealt in great detail with law enforcement, but hardly at all with the developing principles of the law itself, which he tended to avoid throughout his career. This opus was his intellectual monument. In his other books he was at his best when assessing the works of others, always respectfully. I used to wonder whether the hostility which he had experienced in his birthplace - and from contemporary rivals in England, such as Mannheim - had made him cautious about airing new ideas of his own, but if that had been so his very detailed memoirs, *Adventures in Criminology*, published in his nineties, would surely have revealed it. I eventually realised that despite his apparent confidence he was anxious not to make himself ridiculous, and ridicule is what criminological ideas have to face. Sometimes after a speech he would telephone me to ask what impression he had made.

Certainly both Leon and I suffered from political handicaps. Our relations with the Home Office were good, but politicians, the judiciary and the magistracy tended to see criminologists as excusers of criminals rather than impartial scientists. They were right about some criminologists, who were either social workers *manqués* or Marxists who blamed capitalism for most human imperfections. (Yet Marx said nothing worth saying about crime, as Katalin Gonczol, the Hungarian communist, pointed out to my Marxist students.) The irony of the Institute's situation in the seventies, however, was that it was distrusted both by the Right and by the Left. The New Criminologists (as they called themselves) regarded us as the running dogs of the Home Office. My years in the Scottish Home Department made me doubly suspect.

Personal histories apart, however, researchers who valued objectivity were accused of striving for the impossible. Commitment was what mattered. Some of the new criminologists carried out valuable studies of criminal life-styles - sometimes as 'participant observers' - but more popular was the study of police or prison officers. Such research was easier to achieve because most police forces and prisons felt obliged to let themselves be observed at work, whereas criminals didn't. It was as if zoologists had chosen to study the staffs of zoos. I am not denying the value of such enterprises, merely pointing out that police and prison staff are easier game, especially for 'antibodies'.

My arrival at Cambridge coincided with the 1974 election, which led to my last effort to reason with a politician. I was rung up late one evening by Keith Joseph, who wanted to talk about capital punishment, and its value as a deterrent. Under the impression that he was genuinely consulting me, I told him that potential murderers in Britain seem to be deterred (when they are deterred) by 'life' as much as by death, and I suggested that anyway the revival of capital punishment would be popular only with people who would vote Conservative anyway. He reacted with a long speech, as if I were a constituent, and rang off. It reminded me of a new Home Secretary, Robert Carr, whom I had had to introduce to the members of my Advisory Council on Probation. He had prepared himself too thoroughly, and instead of asking questions about the probation service he gave us a short lecture on its aims. I wondered what the point of the meeting was. By way of contrast, when Merlyn Rees consulted me about ways of reducing the prison population he really listened as well as argued.

As for the Institute itself, Leon Radzinowicz had left it well-endowed with first-class staff, recruited for team-work on projects agreed with the Home Office, but the projects and the grants were coming to an end. Teaching had taken second place to research, but this was the beginning of lean years for the Home Office and other sources of funds. Eventually we managed to find other sources of research grants; but at first all I could do was to emphasise to the academic staff that if they could interest any source of money in ideas of their own they would be free to choose their own topics; meanwhile the standard of teaching and examining needed improvement. Good teaching would count as much as good research. I have mentioned their insecurity, and I managed to obtain tenured appointments for several of those whose appointments were not, and eventually to recommend one or two for a readership or a chair.

I was shocked to find that students could get a postgraduate qualification in criminology without any contact with criminals. By coincidence Dermot Grubb, the Governor of Oxford Prison, had been transferred to Bedford, and we soon managed to organise regular student-prisoner seminars on the Oxford lines, compulsory for students but not for prisoners. Even the Cambridge magistrates asked to be allowed to attend these seminars, although their idea of a discussion was rather too didactic. Visiting fellows from abroad were particularly appreciative of the Bedford seminars. They were abandoned after my retirement, by staff who saw more point in zoo-like visits to specialised prisons. Yet some of the newer staff were to be responsible for first-class studies of prisoner-staff relations, prison suicides and prison discipline.

As for undergraduates I found that there was an impression in the Law Faculty that it was the weaker candidates who opted for criminology. With the help of a sympathetic Chairman of Examiners David Farrington and I managed to produce statistics which clearly refuted this. Yet I was also horrified by the variety of topics with which law undergraduates were expected to cope if they opted for criminology, as a great many did. In particular the syllabus included explanations of criminal behaviour, which could be discussed only superficially with undergraduates unacquainted with psychology and sociology. It surprised me that my predecessor, who was of much the same view, had included it in the syllabus, and I took it out.

My own only worthwhile contribution to the explanation of crime was in *Behaviour and Misbehaviour*, which was published soon after I came to Cambridge. I had been struck by the assumption of most sociologists, psychologists and psychiatrists that an explanation of a delinquent act ought to be of a kind that showed why in the circumstances it was inevitable or at least highly probable. A crude determinism, conscious or unacknowledged, was at work. In everyday life, on the other hand, we are often asking for, and content with, the sort of explanation which simply tells us why such behaviour was not psychologically impossible for the individual. When someone unexpectedly loses his temper all we want to know is 'How could he possibly do that?', not 'Why did he have to?' Unless one is faced with someone who repeatedly loses his self-control when most people wouldn't, that is all one is justified in asking for - a 'possibility explanation' not a 'probability' one. And even people who have a tendency to lose their tempers often don't when one would expect it. Recognition of this forestalls a lot of pseudo-explanation. The point appealed more to psychiatrists, whose patients' behaviour is not very predictable; but it made little or no impression on social scientists, some of whom did not grasp its full implications.

Research grants were a worry - when they could be got. One in particular had been overspent by about 100 per cent, by Richard Sparks, an American who conducted the first sound victim-survey in Britain. (He must not be confused with the much younger Richard Sparks, a product of the Institute who did first-class research in prisons.) His brilliance was equalled only by his enjoyment of sabotaging personal relations. It was fortunate for me that the year's interregnum at the Institute had been so competently filled by an acting director, Derick McLintock, whose talent for administration had redeemed the financial situation by the time I took over. (Derick was soon made Professor of Criminology at Edinburgh University, but became addicted to foreign conferences, and died young.) Sparks could not forgive him for saving his bacon, and meetings were soured by his gibes. His sexual exploits, too, were not good for the Institute's reputation. One incident brought him before the magistrates. Late one night a woman who lived alone had been alarmed by someone battering at her door. She telephoned the police, who in those days quite often responded to such calls for help. When she saw them arrive she opened the door, and exclaimed 'Oh, it's only Dr Sparks, constable, that's all right'. To which the constable replied 'It may be all right with you ma'am, but what he said to this policewoman was not all right'. Result: a conviction and fine for being drunk and disorderly. Sparks' assistant lectureship was due to come to an end, and I wanted to be allowed to tell him, before he took a sabbatical at Rutgers, that he would not be welcomed back. I had not realised that employment law would make it so difficult; but eventually I managed it, and we saw no more of him. We heard quite a lot, however. Rutgers gave him a job, but his demon continued to drive him. Drink, fights and eventually drugs led to the sack, and pneumonia killed him.

Having sorted out one or two such problems I enjoyed a six-week sabbatical in Stockholm, which enabled me to visit not only some Swedish prisons but also the Stockholm zoo. I am keen on zoos, and was shocked by Stockholm's. Swedish prisons, on the other hand, were mostly as enlightened as they were said to be. An exception was the high security unit at Kumla where a handful of armed robbers and rapists were confined in very cramped quarters, allowed out of their cells only in threes and fours, so as not to outnumber the warders.

For some time I had hankered after a piece of research which seemed likely to throw empirical light on deterrence. I was able to secure a grant from the Home Office for interviews with young burglars, and to recruit Trevor Bennett, already the co-author of a report on burglary, to lead the project. My other commitments did not allow me to do more than make suggestions - for example showing the young burglars houses of different sorts to see which

126

they chose as targets. Trevor Bennett and his assistant Richard Wright produced a first-class book, *Burglars on Burglary*, and Richard Wright later published two books on burglars and robbers in the USA.

In other respects exchanging Oxford for Cambridge was like stepping back in time. Oxford had - perhaps still has - its dynastic families, who have been dons or wives of dons for generations. Lionel Smith had belonged to one, but escaped. The Butlers were another. Cambridge, however, has families whose names have more resonance: Darwin, Trevelyan, Tennyson. Oxford dons seem less deeply rooted than their Cambridge counterparts. Cambridge colleges are full of men (rarely women) who have been Cambridge schoolchildren, undergraduates, research students and fellows, leaving only for hospital, a sabbatical or Bletchley. College customs favour stay-at-homes by according special privileges to fellows who have been there for most of their lives. Some allow bachelors who have lived in college for, say, 20 years to keep their sets of rooms until they die. Their deaths usually reveal dirt, dry rot and dated pornography. 'Old Cambridge' sees this as mutual loyalty, not stagnation. Old Cambridge saw it as its duty to ensure that its alumni got degrees even if they did no work. Failures were as rare as examiners could make them. They are still rare, but idle students are rare too, now that jobs are scarce.

Cambridge manners are more formal than Oxford's. Soon after our arrival my wife and I were invited to a small dinner-party at a private house. Among the other guests were the Vice-Chancellor and his wife. Quite late in the evening my wife, who was the oldest of the guests, felt that this allowed her to get up and begin our farewells. The Vice-Chancellor's wife commented aloud 'I suppose it's all right to leave before the Vice-Chancellor if it's an informal occasion'. We knew that the rule she had in mind applied to royal guests, but not that it applied to Vice-Chancellors. Perhaps she had in mind that the Chancellor himself was royal. Perhaps she was just new to the job.

Old Cambridge even has ways of talking which distinguish it. For example it is fond of saying 'Oh dear ...' when answering pupils' questions. 'Oh dear ...' means 'Evidently you know less than I thought...' A woman don actually began a letter to me in this way when I asked her where to find the Bills passed by Cromwell's Parliaments. Come to think of it I cannot recall hearing a man use this put-down. It must have been learned in the women's colleges.

Old Cambridge was short-sighted. In the seventies the University Library admitted graduate readers without a pass. One new graduate asked for a pass but was told that there was no such thing: he was free to use the Library without it. He demanded one, and took his case to the central administrators. Even a letter confirming his right to use the Library wouldn't satisfy him. So he stoned the Senate House, more than once. Eventually he was prosecuted and committed to Bedford Gaol, where I saw him wearing a blanket, having proudly refused prison clothing. The poor man was ahead of his time, for the Library was soon compelled by thefts to institute a pass system for all its readers. Perhaps his wish has now been granted.

Does Cambridge have a sense of humour? It has certainly produced comedians, although not many since Peter Cook and his contemporaries flourished. What it doesn't seem to produce is *wits*. Did any of the Apostles say anything witty? When someone objected to a policy on the ground that it mightn't work in the long run Keynes is said to have remarked that in the long run we are all dead; but that was mordant rather than witty. Like most of Cambridge's elite the Apostles took themselves too seriously for wit. It's true that at Trinity Housman was a wit. After his death a notebook was discovered in which he had composed cruel epigrams, with blanks waiting for the names of suitable subjects. He was also a parodist in his less mournful moments:

> "The shades of night were falling fast,
> the rain was falling faster,
> when through an alpine village passed
> an alpine village pastor."

But Housman was a product of Oxford. So too was Bernard Williams, the former Provost of King's: 'The purpose of the oral examination is to make sure that the candidate wrote the thesis'. And has Cambridge ever had a poet like Oxford's Godley, whose comment on a college's new insurance policy was:

> "Well did the amorous sons of Wadham
> their house insure 'gainst fire and flame.
> They knew their crime, the crime of Sodom,
> and judged the punishment the same".

I shall quote Godley again on the subject of examiners.

Cambridge, on the other hand, has fewer chancers than Oxford. I have devoted another chapter to academic impropriety; but here I am talking merely about dons who distinguish themselves by impulsively overestimating their expertise. It was impulsive of my Christ Church contemporary, Trevor-Roper, to authenticate the 'Hitler Diaries', especially when he himself had written an excellent book some years earlier about the fraudulent Sinologist, Sir Edmund Backhouse, who presented the Bodleian Library with forged diaries from the Chinese Imperial Court. It must have been tempting for the author of *The Last Days of Hitler* to accept the invitation to authenticate the crudely forged diary of the Führer; but he should have realised that forensic scientists are now more reliable than historians. I can't think of recent counterparts in

Cambridge, although some of its scientists were equally credulous in the early days of spiritualism and extra-sensory perception.

Cambridge, however, has its own breed of mentally disturbed persecutors. Not long after I arrived I began to get hostile letters from a middle-aged man who lived in a nearby village. He had chosen for his quarrel with me the question whether deterrents ever worked. He believed they never did, a myth that had been fashionable in the sixties. I made the mistake of sending a reasoned reply to the first of his encyclicals, but soon realised that I was dealing with what I call an 'unconvincible'. The letters became rather less frequent - about one every six months - but persisted for 20 years, even after I had retired, although he also tried to pick quarrels with my successors. In spite of these attacks he applied twice for one of the Institute's short-term research fellowships, and on the first occasion asked me to be one of his referees. Fortunately he was ineligible. This suggests to me that he wrote his letters in a hypomanic state, and forgot later how insulting he had been. He enrolled as a reader in the Institute's library, and the staff pointed him out to me, but not me to him, at my request. Recently he has added lecturers and professors at other universities to his list of targets. He refers to himself as a genius, but shows no other sign of delusion, and makes no threats.

A professorship at Cambridge does not automatically guarantee a college fellowship, as it used to do at Oxford. Oliver Zangwill, the psychologist, who liked my books, held out unofficial hope that King's would offer me one, but the first invitation I got was from a less prestigious college. Turning the invitation down was not only a gamble but something that had to be done with tact, and although my excuse was ingenious I can't reveal it without identifying the college. Eventually the hoped-for invitation from King's arrived, and I never regretted the gamble, having been more at home there than I had ever been at Oxford.

The privileges were mainly social - free lunches or dinners in company which could be interesting at times, although modern Cambridge dons feel under no obligation to make conversation at table. In return one was expected to undertake chores. One of these was the job of the Lay Dean. Among his tasks was the traditional obligation to keep an eye open for popery on the part of the ecclesiastical Dean. It seemed sufficient to ask him 'Any popery this term?' But the Lay Dean's chief job was discipline. My predecessors had been young and lax. The bar sold alcohol cheaply in order to encourage undergraduates to drink in college instead of pubs where they were likely to be attacked by the local youth, most of whom seem to be descendants of Boudicca. One result of cheap alcohol was drunken vandalism, but a more serious one was the occasional alcoholic, who could be observed having entirely liquid lunches and dinners. Although I named one or two to the Senior Tutor (and the ecclesiastical Dean when they were choral scholars) he refused to take me seriously until there was a case of *delirium tremens*.

Where drunken vandalism was concerned the worst offender was the Chetwynd Society, founded for literary discussion but by the nineteen-seventies devoted to heavy drinking and late-night roistering - a dismounted equivalent of the Bullingdon Club at Christ Church. By fining individuals, refusing permission for offenders' parties, and in extreme cases forcing them to find lodgings outside I managed to restore a degree of order. I was annoyed to find, however, that my Assistant Dean, who at that time was the Chaplain, was signing permission for Chetwynd Society meetings when I had refused it. Fortunately King's chaplains have short tenure.

I got more help from women undergraduates, who saw no point in connivance or *omerta* when serious damage or intimidation was being investigated. At that time it was a tradition that the college had not within living memory 'sent down' a student, so I never proposed this to the Council. Instead I revived the practice of forcing serious delinquents to live out of college, and enter it only for academic purposes.

One weakness of any college where discipline is concerned is young Fellows who have so recently been students that they still have friends and drinking companions amongst them. There are also Fellows who seem to be natural 'student-lovers', even when they should have grown out of ephebephilia. The state of mind is not necessarily sexual, although King's had for generations been what a *Times* obituarist called 'a centre of gaiety'. From my point of view the trouble was simply that occasionally it would emerge that a really disastrous party, which had resulted in injuries or serious damage, had included one or more Fellows.

The golden age of homosexuality in the college is discussed with insight by Patrick Wilkinson in *A Century of King's*. Even membership of the society called 'The Apostles' was influenced by it.

> "Not without opposition from Trevelyan and others, the idealistic attitude towards homosexual love gave way, under the influence of [Lytton] Strachey and Keynes, to a more sensual pursuit of beautiful young men, even to the point of jockeying to procure their election to the Society" (p.51).

Between the two world wars the college was more than tolerant of what was at that time criminal conduct, although Wilkinson maintains that 'Greek love' in his day - between the wars - was by no means always consummated. He was probably right. In Edwardian and Georgian days many upper-class homosexuals resorted to male prostitutes or 'working-class' men for physical satisfaction. In late modern Cambridge such displacement became unfashionable, but at least one other college now has a reputation gayer than King's. While on this subject it is worth recording that many of the fellows who campaigned for equal status for the women's colleges, and later for the admission of women to men's colleges, were or had been homosexual, and King's was one of the first men's colleges to recruit women as fellows and finally, in 1972, as undergraduates. Women contributed to the decrease in rowdiness, although I hope I helped too.

Another of the problems I had to contend with as Lay Dean was political hysteria. The most striking example was about a young Kingsman who had been irritated by communist notices in one of the college's hostels and, when drunk, had scrawled *Arbeit macht frei* across one of them, outraging not only undergraduates but most Fellows too. My interrogation convinced me that his intention had been jocular rather than inflammatory, but I had to do something formal, so I banned him from the hostel. I then had to face the resignation of an assistant lay dean, who harangued me about my leniency at the Lodge in front of his undergraduate friends. On the other hand I had to receive a deputation from another body of student opinion, which argued that I should have left the culprit to them to deal with. Finally I had to answer to a group of Fellows who wanted an explanation of what seemed to them an inadequate response. They got it, the assistant lay dean's resignation was accepted, and everyone calmed down - all within three days.

Turning out in the middle of the night and driving in to college to deal with trouble in the cellar disco was one of my chores. Undergraduates would stupidly sign in guests from the town whom they did not know, in order to be friendly, but the result was disruptive. Fortunately being middle-aged helped. Even a drunken Scot with a broken bottle (who was nobody's guest) handed it over when I spoke to him in the dialect of our home town, Edinburgh.

On another occasion an undergraduate offered to step outside and take me apart, but thought better of it. A three-year stint as Lay Dean was enough, however. My successor, who disliked the student jungle even more than I did, resorted to professional bouncers, which seemed to me a pity.

One of the pleasures which King's used to provide was lunchtime chess. The young research fellows who could play were hesitant, under the impression that their seniors would regard them as wasting their time. I tried to reassure them, but was never quite sure myself whether I was giving sound advice. So most of my games were with the middle-aged or elderly. After some years, however, it dawned on me that my opponents were dying earlier than mortality statistics would predict as likely. The first to go was Oliver Stallybrass, who was editing the reprints of E.M. Forster's fiction. I came back from a holiday to find that something had driven him to a sudden but planned suicide. One day his assistant, Elizabeth Heine, noticed that he was writing a series of letters, but was unaware that one was addressed to her. By the time she got it he had followed the example of one of his relatives and thrown himself under a train. What distressed her particularly was that she had watched him write to her when he could have spoken.

Another friend, Louis Edwards, had been unable to play for some weeks as a result of what his GP diagnosed as a post-influenzal depression. When we next met for a game, however, I noticed how clumsily he was moving, and suspected that he was suffering from something cerebral. His GP took a lot of persuading to refer him to a neurologist, but sure enough a large tumour was discovered and excised. After that he was occasionally hypomanic, but we continued our companionable games until the tumour reappeared and killed him.

The next chess-playing friend to go was Sir Harry Lintott, a cultivated and amusing man, who had been a High Commissioner

134

in Canada. Later, when the news media were hunting for *The Fourth Man* in the lengthening chain of uncovered spies, his name was bandied about for no better reason than that he had been an Apostle and had known Guy Burgess. I miss both our games and his conversation. He was in his eighties, but the next one to go was in his sixties: Ernest Gellner, the philosopher and anthropologist. He had not long given up his chair at Cambridge to become a professor in his home town, Prague, when he was killed by a heart attack at an airport. I now feel obliged to warn anyone brave enough to play chess with me that I probably have the evil eye. John Daugman, the inventor of eye-screening security devices, gave up chess with me and survives. I have only two opponents left. One of them says the number of deaths is not enough to be significant. The other is in holy orders and may believe he is immune.

The game itself can be 'testy and cholericke ... very offensive to him that looseth the Mate', as *The Anatomy of Melancholy* says. I witnessed an example when, on a sabbatical at Yale, I joined the Newhaven Chess Club one evening. Playing at the next table were a youth and a slightly older man. The elder was losing, and making his moves by banging his pieces on the board. His opponent said 'Come on, you're not in Vietnam now'. The veteran shot to his feet and tried to hit him with his chair. Someone on his right seized the chair in time, and he was calmed down. In Stockholm, again on sabbatical, I used to go down to the Central Library to pick up a game. One evening, however, was spoilt by a man in his thirties who, after losing, tried to provoke me into a fight by a series of crude insults.

12. DEMARCHES AND RESIGNATIONS

"The curfew must not ring tonight"
(Rose Hartwick Thorpe)

So much for King's. In 1980 or thereabouts I made the mistake of accepting the Presidency of the National Association of Probation Officers. Before doing so I consulted Lord Hunt, the retiring President, and asked him why he didn't want to continue. He pleaded new commitments, but I suspect that he had become worried by the attitude of the Association. It seemed to be in opposition not only to any proposal from the Home Office but also to any innovations from any other source, such as the community service order proposed by the Wootton Committee. Its Chairman, Bill Beaumont, was almost as left-wing as it was possible to be, and was the joint author of a book on probation which described the service's primary task as attacking the features of English society which disadvantage petty offenders. 'Socialist probation practice' consisted chiefly of campaigns and 'oppositional work'. Probation officers should keep the minimum of required records, and 'should not wear themselves out'. It's possible that Hunt, who was an idealistic peer, had begun to realise just where the leadership of NAPO was trying to steer it.

NAPO's executive committee may have been a little more moderate than the Chairman, but I never found out because when I asked whether I could attend it as an observer I was told that the President was expected not to, except when invited. My only function was that of a figurehead. I was invited to conferences, and at the Annual General Meeting was expected to give a short winding-up speech. The AGMs' agenda were so full of political and ideological motions that the silent majority of officers didn't attend. Hunt had told me none of this. At times the Association advised its

136

members to strike; but their activities were not missed, even by the news media. When they decided to oppose the idea of curfews for juvenile delinquents I was so fed up with them that in my farewell speech I compared them with the lady in the poem whose Cavalier lover was to be hanged at curfew. This gymnastic lady swung on the clapper of the local church bell, crying 'the curfew must not ring tonight'. The AGM laughed but the activists were not amused, and shortly after that I resigned. I could have 'gone public' with my reasons, but thought that this would be too disloyal.

By this time 10 years of the Directorship also seemed enough. I had only three years left before, at 67, I would have to retire from the Chair, and I had made it clear when forced to accept the Directorship that I regarded it as a coil I could shuffle off before it became mortal. I had spent too much time coping with administration, something I had tried to leave behind me at the Scottish Office. Cambridge administrators had impressed me more than their Oxford counterparts, but some had blind spots. My Institute suffered from a gross instance of bureaucratic amnesia. The endowment which created it had included a large sum for the provision of a building; but the Institute had at first been accommodated in existing buildings, and the Financial Board, having invested the building fund, apparently forgot about it (as did Radzinowicz) so that I did not hear of its existence until after I had retired, by which time inflation had outstripped what was originally a usable sum of money.

Intrigue by dons was childish. A small faction of the Law Faculty wanted to transfer the Institute to the Faculty of Social and Political Sciences, one of the most unruly in the University; but its arguments failed to convince. Again, the University's Library Committee reported to the General Board that the Institute did not need a professional librarian. Their intention was to use the money for another library. Their tactics had been so devious - details would be tedious - that I asked for a review by someone in the role of Ombudsman. This novel request took the administrators aback, but the Vice-Chancellor eventually offered himself, and I persuaded him that the Library Committee had behaved so improperly that its report should be ignored. My threat to publish what had been done in a newspaper may have helped. Anyway he ruled in my favour. But I have devoted another chapter to academic shenanigans, and have said enough here to demonstrate what I was getting tired of.

Early in my time at Cambridge I had been reluctantly made a member of the Council of the Senate, and spent many an exasperating hour debating, for example, whether Cambridge should preserve its nineteenth-century system of making a head of a college its Vice-Chancellor for two years, changing V-Cs as soon as they had become competent, or whether we should copy other universities and appoint whoever seemed suitable for a longer period. It was the decision in favour of the status quo which finally provoked me to resign from the Council. I was told that this had shocked my colleagues, who could not imagine not wanting a seat in the corridors of power. Since most important decisions were made in other committee rooms, a 'corridor' was exactly what the Council was. Maitland described it as 'a body designed to teach men the mortification of the spirit'.

Brutality was sometimes necessary to coerce the administrators. For years the state of our lavatories had been the subject of appeals for refurbishment. Meanwhile the Duke of Edinburgh, as Vice-Chancellor, was familiarising himself with the many institutes in his jurisdiction. One day I was telephoned to ask when it would be convenient for him to visit my institute. Such visits are mere exchanges of courtesies. There was nothing to *see*: we were not a forensic museum. My military experience alerted me to a weak spot, and I replied 'Not until our lavatories are fit for inspection'. They were quickly refurbished, and there has not yet been a royal inspection.

My long-suffering - but effective - successor at the Institute, Tony Bottoms, managed in a more affluent decade what I had not managed, to persuade the University to afford a separate Director; but not until he had spent 14 years coping with administrative demands that were even heavier than in my day. His good fortune was that funds became easier to raise; but raising them involved an enormous amount of paperwork and commuting. When the separate directorship was eventually advertised I was interested to learn that none of the short-listed applicants was British, and I am still unsure why. A possible reason is that the advertised post didn't offer a professorship; but the successful applicant, Mike Tonry, was a distinguished professor from the USA, and was soon made a professor.

Meanwhile I celebrated my retirement by accepting an opportune invitation to lecture at Cape Town University. By what may have been a coincidence I received a letter from the Association of University Teachers urging its members to boycott invitations of this kind from South Africa. It seemed to me that cutting off communication with the liberal half of South African society in this way was short-sighted, and was unlikely to have even the propaganda value which the boycott of cricket tours was supposed to have. So I resigned from the A.U.T. My visit to Cape Town, Johannesburg and Pretoria (where there is a sort of open university which has students all over the Indian Ocean) enabled me to visit several prisons, where I found the staff much more enlightened than propaganda had led me to expect. The police of course were a very different lot. I was most hospitably entertained and made friends whom I still see occasionally. My only criticism of Cape Town University is that its chess club existed only in theory.

By now - the mid-eighties - my nineteen-sixties textbook was obsolete, so on my return I wrote *Sentencing Theory, Law and Practice*, designed to make lawyers reflect about the underlying principles of what some still called 'an art' (see my chapter on myths), but also to make them aware of how sentences were carried out in real life, outside the court-room. A decade later I was fortunate in finding a co-author, Nicola Padfield, to share the production of a second edition.

With more enjoyment, however, I mounted an attack on what seemed to me a pernicious new movement in the USA, called 'Just Deserts'. The book of that name was, ostensibly if not in actuality, the product of a committee of well-known American academics; but the secretary and draftsman was Andrew von Hirsch, who became the prophet of the movement. Its message was that lawbreaking should be punished for Kant's reason: that this was a moral duty. As a matter of historical fact criminal justice systems, and in particular their sentences, are the creations of utilitarians who simply want less crime. The contribution of retributivists has been to insist on some degree of proportionality between the crime and the penalty. The notion that the primary duty of the system is to match evildoing with suffering, whether this reduces evildoing or not, is Kant's legacy to Europe, although in his more realistic lectures Kant himself talked like a utilitarian.

Unfortunately the 'just deserts' movement was encouraged by research, mostly in the USA, which at first cast doubt on the utility of penalties, and particularly on the efficacy of deterrents and correctives. The result was a disillusionment which enabled 'just deserters' to offer their aim as one which was more obviously achievable - a *pis aller* sold as a *nouvelle vague*. It was eventually to inspire a Conservative Home Secretary to introduce a Criminal Justice Act which required prison sentences and community penalties to be 'commensurate with' the offence, although exceptions are allowed, for example for public protection from violent or sexual offenders.

I wrote a short attack on retributivism, called *Why Punish?* which scored a few points (it was also selected for the British National Corpus of contemporary English, which would have impressed old MacRobbie in the Scottish Office). Andrew von Hirsch and I became friends when he joined the Institute of Criminology, and it was noticeable that his later book, *Censure and Sanctions,* offers a more complex justification for penalising crime which is much closer to utilitarianism. The appeal of retributivism, however, is still strong, especially amongst lawyers. In private I am as vindictive as any reader of the *Daily Telegraph* when some particularly evil offender is brought to justice. I simply question whether it is useful or morally justifiable to think in terms of desert rather than deterrence, correction or prevention when sentencing him. This does not necessarily point to a lenient sentencing policy. Jeremy Bentham, the Godfather of utilitarians, could be as tough as any just deserter.

I had always typed my books, but pressure from my daughter and my expert nephew, Michael Potter, persuaded me to convert to a word-processor in my eighties. Like every conversion, it entailed prayer, self-criticism, anxiety and remorse. A major disaster was the crashing of a hard disk at a time when I had roughly drafted most of *Aggravation, Mitigation and Mercy* but had forgotten to keep the floppy disk up-to-date: something I now do every night. I am told that this is a mild example of a machine-induced neurosis.

I am also told that though the Apple empire couldn't salvage the contents of my crashed hard disk the CIA could have; but I didn't know anyone in the CIA. I do remember an American who claimed to be ex-CIA, and who gave me a dinner at a very good restaurant in the hope of a job; but he disappeared, leaving no more than a slight whiff of sulphur. It wasn't corrupt of me, I think, to eat his dinner because I did not realise that he wanted a job until we were drinking coffee.

Perhaps I could have made a more heroic story of my time at Cambridge; but the truth is that it made more demands on my sense of humour than on my courage. My flight from bureaucracy, after plunging me into stressful Nuffield and the anxieties of my first academic job, had eventually landed me in a pleasant, if somewhat complacent, university and a congenial college. Yet just as I had felt not entirely at home in the Academy, Christ Church, the Army and St Andrew's House, it has been in a slightly detached mood that I have experienced academe. Not long ago there was a fashion in sociology for what was called 'participant observation', which meant taking part in what you were studying. I have been a participant observer of academe for the last 40 years. The next two chapters deal in more detail with some of the things I have observed.

13. SOME CRIMINOLOGICAL MYTHS

"... a major cause of crime is the criminal law itself"
(Stan Cohen)

This book is not meant to sell criminology, and will be criticised for not dealing with it more seriously. Criminology has had its myths - what discipline hasn't? - and I am glad to say that I have played a part in disposing of some of them. I have already mentioned the legend - perpetrated or at least endorsed by the social historian Kathleen Jones - that there were no successful insanity defences before Hadfield's trial for firing a pistol at George III in 1800. The myth was probably the result of consulting only the series of reports called the State Trials, which was concerned with cases of national interest, and in which Hadfield's was the first example of a successful insanity defence. In fact the Old Bailey Sessions Papers record many successful defences of this kind in the half-century before Hadfield's case, and the plea rolls in the Public Records Office chronicle occasional examples as early as the 14th century.

But that belongs to legal history. A penological myth is that 'deterrents never work' (I quote from a Howard League letter to *The Times* in the nineteen-seventies). This was consistent with the antipunitive ideology of those days, but had been encouraged, I think, by inferences from studies of capital punishment, from which it appeared that murder-rates were as high in jurisdictions which executed murderers as in those which didn't. The logical inference was of course that potential killers who are in deterrible states of mind are as likely to be deterred by the alternative to the death penalty - i.e. 'life'. In any case it should have been obvious to anyone who tries to park in a city, or who drives more carefully on an icy road, that deterrents sometimes work. Some crimes, however, are committed by people whose state of mind wipes out any thought of consequences. Some people take bigger risks than others, especially with experience. The only justifiable generalisation is that *some types* of deterrent deter *some types* of people from *some types* of crime in *some types* of situation, and not by any means invariably.

But that is history, and other myths are more intriguing. An important one is - or at least used to be - that there is a single cause of crime, or at least a single thing that can be called 'the major cause of crime'. The most vapid assertion of this kind was that 'By definition a major cause of crime is the criminal law itself' (Stan Cohen in *The Listener*). To do him justice he was simply echoing the views of the authors of *The New Criminology*. To do them justice they were inspired by an article in the American journal *Issues in Criminology* for 1970. And to do the authors of that article justice they were inspired by Aristotle.

He distinguished four kinds of cause. A statue, for example, has a material cause (the stone from which it is made), an efficient cause (the sculpting), a final cause (what the sculptor was trying to do), and a 'formal cause', the fact that a statue is a representation of something. The New Criminologists called the criminal law the 'formal cause' of crime. At first sight this is no more than a harmless, if rather precious, way of emphasising that it is a necessary condition of an action's being a crime that it should fulfil the official definition of a crime in the relevant jurisdiction. If one feels that this tautology is dignified by being expressed in the language of Aristotle and Aquinas, is any harm done?

Well yes, if the implication is that the behaviour is made more likely by being defined as a crime, which is what the New Criminologists were implying. This seems contrary to commonsense. If breaking into homes were not a crime, and so not officially punishable, there would be more of it, not less. To do the New Criminologists justice again, there are special situations. In the first place, some types of behaviour are criminalised inadvisedly or unfairly (for example cannabis use or homosexual behaviour). But the law does not cause such behaviour in any modern sense. What is more relevant is that some criminal behaviour is a protest against the specific law that forbids it (as when Sikhs rode motorcycles in turbans to protest against the new requirement to wear crash-helmets), or a protest against some other law (the poll-tax for example). Thirdly, some sociologists claim that 'secondary deviance' is caused by 'labelling' people as 'criminals', thus alienating them from law-abiding people and their values, or making it harder for them to find legitimate employment. Again, some forms of law-breaking are attractive just because they risk arrest and its consequences: joy-riding in other people's cars is the obvious example.

The New Criminologists may have been trying to emphasise a fifth point: that there are a lot of things which people do inevitably, but which societies for one reason or another (religious, economic, and so forth) are ill-advised enough to discourage by means of the criminal law, thus creating criminals. I called this 'Eden-ideology', because it is so reminiscent of Genesis Chapter 3, in which Adam and Eve are happy and harmless nudists until criminalised by the knowledge of good and evil. It scarcely seems relevant when one is talking about murder, rape, robbery and such goings-on.

The New Criminologists made more valuable contributions than this, although I used to call them 'the as-good-as-new criminologists' because so many of their points were not quite new. More interesting from a psychological point of view were other monolith-makers. John Stuart Mill took the commonsense view that the same phenomenon could be due sometimes to one cause, sometimes to another. Durkheim, the French sociologist, could not accept this: *a un même effet correspond toujours une même cause.* Suicide was awkward, because it seemed to have several causes;

but he got round that by subdividing suicide into different sorts. Yet his sociological followers persisted in trying to find what I called 'the criminologist's stone' - a monolithic explanation of 'Crime'. It was as if physicians were convinced that 'Disease' must have a single explanation because it has a generic name. Psychologists, notably the great and much maligned Cyril Burt, insisted on the multiplicity of factors which contributed to delinquency, and a few sociologists, including Robert Merton, saw the futility of trying to formulate a single explanation; but other well-known social scientists were more optimistic. Wilkins even offered 'a general theory of deviance' to explain non-criminal behaviour as well as crime. Working-class values, insecurity, moral drift, an unconscious desire for punishment, are other examples. The last is particularly interesting, because it illustrates the fate of so many *aperçus*. Freud said that some criminals suffered from unconscious guilt which made them do punishable things in order to be punished. Edward Glover, a minor Freudian of the mid-century, generalised this, and called it 'the key to the problem of delinquency'. But the field called criminology is littered with these old monoliths, embellished with the graffiti of intellectual sightseers.

I had supposed, when I began a short sabbatical at Yale Law School in 1974, that in my post-graduate class on explanations of crime there would be no need to do more than mention this historical curiosity. I was horrified to find that the postgraduate law-students in my seminars - the cream of the new generation - were almost unanimously convinced that there must be a monolith, and wanted me to lead the way to it. I got so heated at this seminar that as it broke up I apologised, whereupon a bright girl said 'well, at least you *cared*'. Her name was Hillary Rodham, and I heard later that she had married another less articulate student in the class, Bill Clinton.

It was about this time that feminism began to point out its

relevance for criminology. It made valid points, of course, but some of its by-products were ridiculous. An example was the assertion that the rapist is the man next door (reasoning which would make the mother next door an infanticide). More harm, however, was done by amateur statisticians. One of them noticed that if female and male prisoners are compared, higher percentages of the females have no previous convictions. His inference was that criminal courts were dealing more severely with women than with men; and he published this nonsense. I hastened to point out that in the whole population of men and women fewer of the latter had previous convictions, a difference one would expect to find reproduced in most kinds of sample. No inference about the severity of sentencing could be drawn. If he had sampled probationers instead of prisoners he would have found a similar disparity. More professional studies have confirmed that women are less likely (and never more likely) than men with similar records to be sentenced custodially. It is said that this may not be true of serious violence; but I have noticed that women who hire hit-men to kill their partners are almost always sentenced more lightly than the hit-men. But the prison-based myth persists, and was solemnly invoked in 1998 by the National Association of Probation Officers. It even appears in Helena Kennedy's book, *Eve was Framed*.

Other kinds of campaigner encourage other sorts of myth, and are able to sell them to journalists. An example is the myth that people who are tried but acquitted, or better still convicted but have their convictions quashed, are always 'innocent'. As that eminent criminal lawyer, Louis Blom-Cooper, has pointed out in a forceful book, the most that can be said in the majority of cases is that the high standard of proof required made a conviction 'unsafe'; but what is unsafe is not necessarily - nor even probably - mistaken. It is an unfortunate feature of English criminal procedure that a jury has to choose between 'guilty' and 'not guilty'. The Scottish verdict of 'not proven' is a third choice, but is falling into disuse, and in any case is not a perfect solution. What courts should have is a choice between at least three verdicts - 'probably innocent', 'not proven guilty', and 'guilty beyond reasonable doubt'. Even that may not be quite enough. Mercy killings trouble juries when the accused is unable to offer any recognised defence (such as diminished responsibility). Even if judges were not obliged to sentence murderers to 'life' that would not avoid the stigma of being convicted of murder. A verdict of 'guilty but morally justified' is not unthinkable.

Another favourite of over-simplifiers is 'the presumption of innocence'. Innocence is 'presumed' only while the trial of guilt is proceeding, and is simply a rhetorical way of saying that justice requires convincing evidence of guilt before a finding of guilt. Yet it is often invoked as an objection to arrests based on suspicion, or to the refusal of bail for good reason, or even to unofficial precautions, all based on mere probabilities. I shall say more about this in my chapter on innocence.

A windmill which troubles retributivists - and not only retributivists - is the nature of responsibility, criminal or moral. Scots lawyers used to talk of 'mental responsibility' for acts as if it were something like intelligence. Psychiatrists, jurisprudes and philosophers wrote books about it, usually trying to define it in terms of concepts such as rationality. This seems unnecessary, since it can be defined very simply as 'having no acceptable excuse for one's act or omission'. The usual excuses are accident, mistake, delusion, idiocy, senility, duress, necessity, justification (real or imagined), automatism (as in sleep) and mental immaturity. What is an acceptable excuse varies from one penal or moral code to another: 'superior orders' are an example. Some things are accepted as partial excuses: for instance provocation. The error was to hunt for a positive definition of responsibility when a negative one fits better. It was like treating black as a colour when it is really an absence of colour. 'Responsibility' is the phlogiston of jurisprudence. (I am not of course talking about the causal sense of 'responsible' in which rain is said to be responsible for floods. As for talking about 'a responsible sort of person' all it means is 'the sort of person who does not usually need to find excuses for his acts or omissions'.)

A myth for which psychiatrists were responsible is that men who merely expose themselves hardly ever attempt a more serious sexual offence. When Sarah McCabe and I studied the careers of a large sample of men committed to mental hospitals for this offence we found that about a third of them either had more serious sexual offences in their records or committed them after discharge from hospital, and a study of the American literature revealed similar findings. What is probably true is that some convictions for indecent exposure should have been for some more serious offence, such as an attempt at an indecent assault, but that the evidence was not quite sufficient to prove anything worse. No doubt there are flashers who are content with flashing, but it needs a very thorough investigation to make it safe to assign one to this category.

A popular and pretentious *dictum* in judges' autobiographies is that sentencing is an art. It should not be necessary nowadays to dispose of this, but it persists, especially in autobiographies. To call an activity an art has two implications: that it calls for originality and that the effect has aesthetic value. Obviously neither is true of sentencing. The sentences which judges are allowed to pass are defined by statute. Judges in some jurisdictions of the USA can sometimes improvise - for example by requiring cannabis growers to carry labels in public, but not in Britain. As for ascribing aesthetic value to a sentence, this might have been plausible when penalties were such as to titillate Swinburne, but there is nothing aesthetic about imprisonment, community service or a fine. What judges seem to mean is that choosing between different types of sentence is a special kind of *skill*, in which so many variables have to be taken into account that it can't be communicated by mere instruction, rather like crossword solving. In reality most sentences are more or less dictated by recognised limits or by the Court of Appeal. In a few cases the judge feels obliged to hesitate between a custodial and a non-custodial disposal, and may feel proud of his eventual decision. The statistics suggest, however, that in terms of reconviction the effects of the two choices are so similar that his choice is immaterial, although of course community service is both cheaper and less likely to do damage than a prison sentence. Genuine skill can make an important difference when there is a possibility that an offender will do grave harm to someone if not properly restrained or supervised; but in such cases a wise judge relies on expert advisers.

This reminds me of the old myth about dangerousness. In the sixties it was fashionable to discredit the label 'dangerous' when applied to offenders. Even etymology was invoked to show that the word 'danger' originated from a word meaning 'power', although the relevance of this was hard to explain. More to the point, psychiatrists such as Peter Scott said that there were no dangerous people, 'only dangerous situations', the implication being that such situations were preventable, and that violent or sexual offenders should not be detained any longer than was necessary for treatment or deterrence. There were two weaknesses in this argument. Non-custodial supervision cannot be relied upon to shield violent people from provocation or sexual offenders from temptation. More important, while it is true that most violent or sexual offences are reactions to situations, some offenders seem to find themselves in provocative or tempting situations much oftener than can plausibly be attributed to chance, and a few clearly plan and contrive to create the necessary situations. I call them the 'opportunity-seekers' or 'opportunity-makers'.

An even more spurious argument was based on statistics. It is a *minority* of violent offenders who repeat their offences. To detain them solely in order to protect others is therefore to make more mistakes than would be made by releasing them. If only one violent man in three is going to commit another violent crime, then releasing all three makes only one mistake instead of two. This verbal sleight of hand is achieved by the use of the word 'mistake' to refer to two very different things - a decision to detain in a case in which this may be unnecessary, and a decision to release which leads to another victim. You cannot put detention and tragedy in the same pair of scales. What I did also point out, however, was that if an offender (or hospital patient) is being detained solely for the protection of others - i.e. longer than is justified by other considerations - he is owed some sort of recompense, which should take the form of living conditions which are as tolerable as resources and security will allow.

Whether sentencing is an art or not, another traditional belief of judges is that their sentences influence the attitudes of the public to the offences in question: a tradition which is at least a century old. It seemed to me that it needed to be tested. With the help of Catherine Marsh, an expert on sampling and survey design who died a few years later, sadly young, I designed a survey which used a number of faked newspaper cuttings with descriptions of interesting offences of dishonesty and violence. The cases had to be of a kind in which (a) either probation or a short prison sentence would seem plausible to the ordinary citizen and (b) his or her moral judgments were likely to vary.

The "Newspaper Cuttings"

Ex-Boxer breaks Challenger's Jaw

A broken jaw was the result of a challenge to a fight outside a Northtown public house. But the man who challenged Robert Brown (30), did not know he had been a welterweight boxer. Brown pleaded guilty to causing actual bodily harm outside the Rose and Crown. He told the court he thought the other man knew he was a boxer.

Computer Fraud Exposed

A bank employee who cheated thousands of customers by using his computer skills was brought to book in court yesterday. Sidney Smith (30) pleaded guilty to stealing more than £7,000 by instructing the computer to deduct any odd pence from cheques paid into customers' accounts and pay them into his own account. On his behalf counsel pointed out that his system ensured that no single person suffered serious loss.

TELEPHONE VANDAL CAUGHT

A man who smashed up telephone kiosks when he could not get his calls through was identified by a traffic warden who was waiting to make her own call from a box. Pleading guilty to criminal damage, Robert Jenkins (20) said he lost his temper when his girlfriend's office refused to put him through to her.

The Case of the Hungry Husband

Gossiping with her neighbours all day ended in violence for a Scottish housewife in Westville when her husband came home to find the house dirty and no meal ready for him.

"She had all day to get me a meal ready and clean the place up a bit" said Bertram Wilson (24), who pleaded guilty to assaulting his wife. "It wasn't the first time, and I just lashed out." Mrs Wilson sustained a cut lip, requiring a stitch.

The Booby-Trapped Greenhouse

Arthur Jackson suffered so many thefts of plants and tools from his greenhouse that he booby-trapped it, injuring a teenage thief.

Pleading guilty to causing actual bodily harm, Jackson (31) said that after putting up with repeated thefts from his greenhouse over a period of years he fixed up a piece of timber so that it would fall on anyone who opened the door without inserting a peg. Two nights later he heard a crash and found a boy lying in the greenhouse, with a cut in his head that required three stitches. The boy admitted several thefts from the greenhouse.

Using professional interviewers we showed these to about 1200 adult respondents in the north and south of England. The cuttings did not specify the sentences for the offences: nowadays offenders are often remanded for sentencing at a later date. Some respondents were told that the offender had been put on probation, others that he had received a short prison sentence. Other respondents were told that the judge had strongly condemned the offence, others again that he had expressed a tolerant view. None of these variations seemed to influence respondents' moral evaluations of the offence. The respondents whose evaluations *were* influenced were those who were told instead the views of 'people like yourself' in a (fictitious) survey. This demonstrated that, while a 'band-wagon effect' could be achieved in this way, neither judges' views nor their sentences influenced people's moral judgments. Even a cumulative effect of repeated sentencing is unlikely, since the news media don't handle sentencing in that way. These findings, published in more than one place, have never been challenged. Yet jurisprudes and sociologists have persisted in claiming that one of the justifications for penalties is their educative effect on the public.

The harm done by imprisonment is not exactly a myth but has been so much exaggerated that it is worth mention. Physical harm can certainly be inflicted, especially if one belongs to an unpopular minority, such as sexual offenders or corrupt policemen. The risk of contracting HIV is exaggerated, unless one is a needle-using drug addict; but the risk of hepatitis is not. What is most often exaggerated is the 'institutionalisation' of which Goffman accused mental hospitals and prisons. Goffman himself had worked in a mental hospital, but drew for much of his 'evidence' on what he had read about concentration camps, nunneries, military barracks, boarding schools and other extreme environments. Later Stan Cohen and Laurie Taylor published a book, *Psychological Survival*, which was based on their discussions with long-term prisoners in a the high-security wing of Durham Prison. They had been allowed there as teachers, but introduced the prisoners to literature about the deadening effects of imprisonment. They then found that the prisoners thought that their mental states were deteriorating.

It so happened that psychologists from Durham University were studying the prisoners by means of psychometric tests, although *Psychological Survival* rubbished this approach. The tests suggested that the prisoners' mental skills were not deteriorating (indeed they had become more articulate); but Cohen and Taylor reported that the prisoners felt they were. What seems likely is that their fears of deterioration were inspired by the literature with which they had been supplied and by the discussions with Cohen and Taylor, who clearly believed in institutionalisation. When I met one of their subjects - MacVicar, the famous robber - after his release, he indignantly rejected the suggestion that he had deteriorated. His later achievements included two university degrees. In any case it has never been shown that the psychological effects of detention in non-extreme conditions are irreversible. Even released lifers are usually able to live normal lives without assistance. The safest employee is a released domestic murderer. But such exaggerations suit the critics of incarceration, especially when supported by biased research.

As for the belief that prisons are 'schools for crime', which was popularised by Sydney Smith in 1821, it is supported by the autobiographies of one or two ex-prisoners - who may have been trying to justify their recidivism - but not by any research. Ex-prisoners are no more likely than ex-probationers to be reconvicted, when allowances are made for age, type of offence, previous convictions and other relevant characteristics. What must be distinguished, of course, are the learning of new techniques and skills, and the acquisition of delinquent values and attitudes from new friends. The techniques one learns in prisons are - as prisoners in my seminars pointed out to me - the techniques which have landed them inside. If so, they have merely become easier to identify and convict. As for the acquisition of criminal attitudes, it occurred to me not long ago that there is at least one category of prisoner who is unlikely to have such attitudes before incarceration, and that is men imprisoned for driving offences who have no criminal records. Mike Hough and I therefore compared samples of dangerous drivers who had either been given short prison sentences or dealt with non-custodially. A two-year follow-up revealed few reconvictions, and no more for the ex-prisoners than for the non-custodial sample. None of the ex-prisoners, for example, had been convicted of drug offences, whereas nine of the non-custodial group had. There was no evidence that short terms of imprisonment had steered the dangerous drivers into crime. Whether long terms do has still to be determined; and it isn't easy to devise research which will tell us.

Debunking myths and exaggerations is fun, but unpopular fun. It usually means treading not only on people's reputations but also on ideological toes. It is less creative and less impressive than devising new hypotheses, but every hypothesis needs to be tested. Even the supreme debunker, Sir James Jeans, did no harm to biology when he said 'Life is simply a disease of matter in its old age'.

14. ACADEMIC SHENANIGANS

"Here lies a poor examiner;
of life he grew aweary.
So let the legend on his tomb be ß-?"

(Godley)

Myth-making is one thing: shenanigans are another, and more entertaining. Just as town-dwellers are cheered by the occasional glimpse of wild life - a fox at their rubbish-bins, for example - my spirits have been refreshed form time to time by the news, or personal observation, of academic sinfulness. I don't mean the sort of sinfulness in which ordinary human beings can indulge - adultery, shoplifting, slander, violence, vandalism or tax evasion. I mean the sort which can be committed only if you are engaged in research, teaching or examining.

Examining may not seem an opportunity for enjoyable sin. Some examiners are merely bored and negligent, or incapable of appreciating brilliance. Some examiners however are corrupt. There are different sorts of corruption, and the taking of bribes is only one. The Oxbridge college system encourages a less sordid sort: the desire to help candidates from one's own college. In the days when candidates' names were on their papers I have been at examiners' meetings at which candidates on the borderline between two classes were helped across no-man's-land by tacit cease-fires (I hesitate to suggest they were explicit). Even in later years, when candidates were identified only by numbers, some internal examiners broke the code. There was even a consensus in one faculty that whatever his college a candidate should not be failed. I have heard external examiners express real disquiet after such meetings. I wish they had done so officially, as was their duty.

Some examiners are even capable of giving improper assistance to candidates from their own colleges. A faculty board of which I was a member was told one summer term of a rumour current among undergraduates. An examiner had been giving closed seminars to candidates from his own college, on subjects which, according to the rumour, turned out to be very relevant to some of the questions in the examination paper he was setting. The faculty board was at first inclined to dismiss the rumour as something of which it could take no official notice; but it seemed outrageous to me that there should be no attempt to verify the rumour. I pointed out that it would not look well if the rumour ever became the subject of publicity, and it became known that the board had been told of it but had done nothing about it. The Chairman reluctantly agreed to talk to the examiner concerned, and simply reported at the next meeting that he had done so.

Examiners of theses are supposed to rely on their own expertise. I co-examined, however, with one who didn't. I was surprised at the time when I found that he had had himself appointed as internal examiner, because the subject of the thesis lay outside his specialism. I think that, having been instrumental in securing an appointment for the candidate, he wanted to make sure that the thesis was accepted without serious criticism. He first persuaded me, against the regulations, to sign a joint report (reports were required to be independent, but he had told me that this rule was no longer enforced). At the oral examination I questioned the candidate, after which my co-examiner read out a series of excellent, penetrating questions from a sheet of paper. The candidate answered them all skilfully. My co-examiner then turned over the sheet of paper, and before he could turn it back again I glimpsed one more typed question, followed by 'Yours sincerely' and a signature. After dinner that evening I said to him that I had been impressed by his questions, and would like to look at them at leisure; but he wouldn't part with the piece of paper.

But that was at Cambridge. Almost as soon as I arrived in Oxford I had been placed in a difficult position. The Faculty Board of Law asked me to reexamine a D.Phil. thesis, written by an Iraqi judge. Its subject was the impact of the Code Napoleon on Bedouin tribal laws. It had been supervised by my predecessor, Max Grunhut, and was rather interesting. The degree committee of the Law Faculty had had predictable difficulty in finding examiners for this extremely exoteric subject. Eventually they had resorted to the Reader in Arabic, although no knowledge of the language was required to understand the thesis. As external examiner they chose a man who had been a public prosecutor in Aden, which was believed to be close enough to Iraq. Conscious no doubt that neither knew anything about Iraq the examiners had proceeded to find as many trivia to criticise as they could, but said that the thesis was acceptable. How could this be, in view of all their criticisms, asked the Faculty Board. The thesis must be reread.

By this time the judge had returned to Baghdad, and the Master of his college had written to him to say that he was sorry he had not been able to bid him a personal farewell. A harmless courtesy; but he added that he was glad that the judge's time at Oxford had been so well spent. The judge had very reasonably taken this to mean that his thesis had been accepted, and had thrown a party which was the talk of Baghdad.

I found it difficult in these circumstances to appraise the thesis with complete detachment. It was my first introduction both to the Code Napoleon and the customary laws of the Bedouin, to say nothing of the customary laws of Oxford. In these difficult circumstances I did what I saw as my duty. After all the thesis was certainly a contribution to knowledge, and most of the examiners' criticisms were rather trivial. I reported that I had found no compelling reason to argue against their conclusion that the thesis was acceptable. The judge got his D.Phil. It was not until 40 years later that I told the story to one of Grunhut's research assistants, who said 'Well I should hope so: I put in a lot of work on that thesis'.

Overconscientiousness is one thing: bias is another. I recall having to point out to one external examiner that not only some but all the questions in her paper could be answered only by a Marxist or a Marxisant mimic. Equally wicked is the examiner who insists that a thesis must accord with his own views, or be revised until it does. In a flagrant case of this kind the relevant degree committee agreed with me that the examiner be thanked and replaced.

I am not sure whether what follows is an example of bias or scruple. London University had - perhaps still has - a questionable convention that a doctoral candidate's supervisor is usually his internal examiner. Since rejection of the thesis would - or at any rate should - reflect on the supervisor it is obviously in his interest that the thesis be accepted, if possible without being 'referred back' for revision. I was once asked to arbitrate between an internal examiner who regarded the thesis as acceptable and an external examiner who didn't. The unfortunate candidate had planned a sound piece of research which was based on the reasonable assumption that the Prison Department would not change its system for allocating young men to different borstals, at least while he was sampling them. Unfortunately the Prison Department did just that, and the man's supervisor had let him continue his research. The external examiner thought that he shouldn't have, and that the thesis should fail. They reached no agreement after the oral examination.

By the time I was asked to arbitrate the candidate was on the point of flying back to his own country, and I had to give him his second oral examination in the station hotel at Paddington. In a way both examiners were right. The change in the allocation system meant that the findings of the thesis were not a reliable 'contribution to knowledge' - only *probably* so. On the other hand the supervisor had rightly regarded the man's method as sound, his work as thorough, and the thesis as well presented. I took the view that since the supervisor had taken the responsibility for allowing him to carry on the candidate should not suffer. But I had, if possible, to persuade the two examiners to agree on a verdict. I gave them a college dinner and a lot to drink after it. Around midnight the external examiner weakened. I had two reports in my drawer, one of which said that we were all agreed on the acceptability of the thesis, the other said that we weren't, but that I had sided with the internal examiner. The external examiner took up his pen to sign the unanimous version. At this precise moment the internal examiner gave an exclamation of triumph. The external examiner threw down his pen and refused to sign. The candidate got his Ph.D. by a mere majority.

There are ordinary burglaries and academic burglaries. Some burglaries make history. A lawyer who had been a DA in Washington told me that the Watergate scandal began with a telephone call to him in the middle of the night from a police sergeant who said 'Sir, we got a kinda unusual burglary down here'. Our burglary at the Institute of Criminology was also kind of unusual, and made a little piece of local history. One December day an observant cleaner noticed a few fragments of putty outside the Administrative Secretary's door, and found that an entire pane of glass had been neatly removed from the transom above the door. Miss Guy, the Administrative Secretary, at once suspected that the burglar had been trying to find the paper for the 'screening' examination which candidates were due to sit in two days' time, at the end of their first term. Yet we could find no sign that he had been able to open the locked filing cabinet where the paper was. We decided not to alter the paper. No candidate did suspiciously well. One did rather badly, and was warned that we hoped the quality of his work would improve. His second-term essays were just acceptable, but his final dissertation was appalling. This was surprising, because he had come to us with an impressive degree in psychology from a South African university. On being told of his failure he had an interview with me. I explained that the regulations did not allow him to retake the examinations, and that medical excuses were usually accepted only if supported by certificates before the end of the course.

A few days later Miss Guy's office was burgled again. The candidate had appealed to the Board of Graduate Studies, saying that he had been under psychoanalytic treatment for domestic problems, and that he had sent his supervisor a letter to this effect on the 14th of February, halfway through the course. His supervisor had in fact never received a letter about this psychoanalytic treatment, but one was found in the candidate's file in Miss Guy's filing cabinet. We later learned that this type of filing cabinet can be opened unobtrusively by unscrewing the back. Meanwhile the Board of Graduate Studies had caused the Degree Committee to hold an inquiry, as a result of which the candidate was generously allowed to revise his dissertation. An examiner who knew nothing about the situation was needed, and I invited Professor John Gunn from the London Institute of Psychiatry. As soon as he heard the candidate's name he told us that this man had been expelled from Gunn's course for having bogus references and degrees. The Board of Graduate Studies were incensed, and told the police, who raided the man's lodgings and found more than one passport, plus unused stationery with the headings of several prestigious institutions. He spent some months in Bedford gaol, and then disappeared. He was a well-spoken man, and I have no doubt has done well somewhere.

A bogus degree does not necessarily mean that the candidate is worthless. I recall being told of a man who was accepted as a postgraduate student by Oxford, claiming a degree from another university. He married an Oxford girl, but the marriage was found to be bigamous, and the discovery led to the unmasking of his non-existent degree. Yet his supervisor swore that he was extremely knowledgeable about his subject, a very specialised branch of European history, and would certainly have got a postgraduate degree. Instead he emigrated to Canada, where he contracted a third marriage. By a twist of fate this turned out to be a valid one, for his first wife had died without his knowledge, and his second marriage was no marriage. He moved on, however, always westward, until he came full circle. When I told this story at dinner one night in another English university a historian said 'Yes, and he now does a little quite satisfactory teaching here'.

Sometimes the motives of these impostors are simply economic. They want to qualify themselves for a teaching job. Sometimes it is more pathological. Some of the *soi-disant* surgeons, gynaecologists or general practitioners who have no formal qualifications have chosen their roles because they are attracted by the drama, by the freedom to handle flesh, or by sadism. I believe that some academic impostors are attracted by what they see as the social standing of university teachers. They must be living in the past, but they don't know that.

Plagiarism is as old as science, and probably as old as the Bible - witness the stories of Noah and Gilgamesh. Ptolemy the astronomer lifted a lot of his celestial observations from Hipparchus of Rhodes. Apparently they were fairly accurate if Rhodes was where you were lying on your back, but not if you were supine in Alexandria. Ptolemy's unacknowledged debt seems to have been suspected at the time, but by writers who didn't seem to be scandalised. Europeans have been more censorious, at least since Elizabethan times. Copyright became legally protected two hundred years ago, but it is possible to plagiarise without infringing it, and especially in academic examinations and dissertations.

My own experiences of plagiarism have been minor, involving students. At Berkeley (where by the way, even as early as the sixties one could buy an essay or even a short dissertation from an agency) I had a class of graduates, each of whom had to submit an essay for discussion. One essay began with a strikingly well-expressed passage, but got worse. I traced the passage and faced the student with the original. His excuse was that he had simply been negligent with quotation marks; but it was a very long quotation. Unintentional plagiarism is not of course impossible: witness the example documented below.

ERRATUM

The article entitled "[. . . . .]" in Volume 6, No. 2, Summer 1971, and which appeared under my name requires a correction of authorship.

An unauthorised paper was given to me by a partner with whom I worked on a project. I sued this paper with only editorial adaptation. I now know that the paper was written by Dr. . . . ., ..., while he was a graduate student at . . . .

I am publicly acknowledging that Dr. . . . . was the author of the article and wish that all future bibliographic references to the article be recorded as follows: . . . .
. . . .
. . . .
. . . .

I am ordering reprints with the corrected attribution to be sent to the entire mailing list of the journal and hope that henceforth all references to this article will be recorded as indicated in the reprint.

. . . .

At my own Institute, but after my retirement, a first-term essay by a graduate student seemed oddly uneven. The internal examiner was critical of half of it, but praised the other half. The candidate was unlucky, for the other half had been written by the external examiner, but an admission of guilt earned her a mere reprimand. Less fortunate was a candidate for a master's degree in a quite different subject. All his written work had been satisfactory, with the exception of a long essay in which an examiner detected long plagiarised passages. I do not know how severe the examiners would have been if he had confessed his sin. As it was he maintained that someone had maliciously substituted the plagiarising essay for the one he had really submitted. Unfortunately for him his supervisor had xeroxed some pages of the essay before it was submitted, in order to discuss them with him, and the copies were clearly from the plagiarising essay. His appeals - to the Septemviri and later to the Divisional Court - were unsuccessful, and he did not get his degree.

Nicely debatable was the behaviour of a student who attended Dr Dias' well organised lectures on jurisprudence. He took such careful notes that after graduating he was able to publish a text-book on the subject. The lecturer's complaint led to an inquiry, and the republication of the book with an amended authorship. The story is a warning to lecturers to publish what they have to say - if it is original - before someone else does. They cannot very well argue that their listeners should be prohibited from publishing on their subject as long as they are lecturing on it.

Cheating in examinations is technically easier than it used to be. I've been told that hearing-aids can be used in favourable buildings, which seems to be confirmed by my own experience with my first hearing-aid. It was built into a pair of glasses, and its circuitry included a six-inch wire leading from one ear to the other. I had left the Oxford Street clinic which had fitted me with it when suddenly an irritated voice said in my ear 'Bryanston Square? Bryanston

Square? ...' It was a frightening few seconds before I realised that I was not experiencing a hallucination but hearing a taxi-driver's radio.

Cheating by students is too common to be interesting, however, and is so much a fact of life that in the USA manuals for preventing it - and for perfecting it - are on sale in bookshops. Detected cases are now dealt with leniently at many universities (but not Cambridge). More interesting is dishonest research. Two friends of mine fell victims to it. Both had, for different periods, employed what they believed to be an experienced interviewer to administer questionnaires, in substantial numbers, to samples of the public. One employer - the late John Martin - was particularly impressed with the man's thoroughness. Interviewees often respond in ways that are hard to classify, and John Martin was constantly being asked by this interviewer to resolve problems of this kind. It was some time before he learned from my other friend that some of this man's interviews had probably never taken place. When tackled the interviewer admitted having filled in most of John Martin's questionnaires while sitting in his riverside cottage. A considerable number of questionnaires had to be scrapped. Those were the early days of surveying. The danger is now familiar to market research firms, whose supervisors detect fakers by random follow-ups, after which the fakers are blacklisted.

Wholesale faking is rare, but an example came my way when I was on the editorial board of the *British Journal of Criminology*, and had to 'referee' an article by a psychologist who had taken part in an experiment at a community home for delinquent boys. The Principal of the home had devised a regime for improving their social attitudes, but adopted it only in one of his houses, to which boys were randomly allocated, the old regime being preserved in the other house. The psychologist had used a well-tried questionnaire to measure attitude-change, and the Principal had asked for a copy. Some time later the Principal published a book which reported the success of his new regime, as measured by the psychologist's questionnaire. This had astonished the psychologist, whose findings over the same period had been that if anything it was the old regime that had resulted in more improvement. Nor did the numbers of his subjects correspond with the Principal's. The article submitted by the psychologist told the whole story in convincing detail; but the *Journal* could not afford to risk a libel action. The psychologist readily agreed to adopt a more careful wording, and to send the article to the Principal for comments. None were forthcoming. We admired the final words of the article, and published it:

> "X's book is of interest because the Principal of a community home has gone out of his way to use a scientific approach to study the effects of his treatment ... and to publish the results. It is also of interest because the results he published are at odds with those of a scientist who was collecting data in the same institution, on the same variables, at the same time, without knowing that the Principal was replicating his work or that he was replicating the Principal's work."

It is all too probable, however, that more people read the book than the article.

Academic appointments used to be the targets of much criticism. The suspicions were usually of nepotism, or more precisely what is now called 'cronyism'. Fairly close to literal nepotism however (the Popes' 'nephews' being usually their sons) was the appointment of a Scot whom I knew to the chair just vacated by his father. It is conceivable that the father took care not to influence the decision: but the son was by no means an obvious choice, having published little.

By the time I reached Oxbridge the filling of senior posts there was fairly strictly controlled. The holder could not be a member of the appointing committee, although he could write a reference for the candidate he favoured, and there was no way of preventing him from being consulted. Nor was there any way of making sure that the committee did not include a saboteur. When Oxford was trying to appoint its first Reader in Sociology several of the candidates were well qualified; but some dons did not regard sociology as a subject which Oxford should encourage (much the same had happened when English was first proposed as an academic subject). The anti-sociologists were ably represented on the committee by Max Beloff, whose views should have made him ineligible. He managed to disparage every candidate on the short list, and persuaded the committee to recommend none of them: an unjustifiable insult to all of them. Oxford did eventually fill the readership, but only after antagonising several sociologists who would have graced the post.

I myself witnessed a variation of the Beloff gambit, this time involving a chair. Another member of the selection committee telephoned me privately with the suggestion that nobody on the short list was really up to standard, and that we should put forward the name of X, a man we both knew. I was outraged. Not only had X not applied, but his subject was on the fringes of criminology. Several of the other candidates were better qualified. I persuaded her not to pursue the idea.

An example of what might be called a negative shenanigan is the way in which some doctoral candidates are treated. Some are accepted by universities who have nobody competent to supervise them. This can be justified only if a competent supervisor can be found at a nearby university, or if - as occasionally happens - the would-be candidate is obviously an expert in his chosen subject. Some supervisors take their responsibilities very lightly. My daughter submitted her draft thesis of some 300 pages to her supervisor at the Maudsley Hospital only to have it returned with no comments - only one or two spelling corrections. Almost as deplorable was the lackadaisical way in which doctoral theses were - and for all I know still are - handled at Cambridge when they had been submitted for examination. Most doctoral candidates need jobs as soon as possible, and need their Ph.Ds to get them. An efficient supervisor would get the relevant Degree Committee to recommend the names of examiners in advance, but this did not guarantee that the examiners would give it priority. Some would accept in spite of being involved in other examinations. Some were just dilatory. Eventually the Board of Graduate Studies instructed examiners to aim at holding the oral examination within two months, but did nothing to ensure that they did, so that some candidates had to wait for no less than half a year. Worse still, even if all went smoothly, and examiners reported on time, their report might arrive at the Board's office in vacation. It could lie there for most of August, all September, and the first week of October because the Board itself did not meet during that period. If the examiners required any serious revision it might be two wasted months before the candidate was told. I protested to the Chairman of the Board, but nothing was done, although it may have been in the years since my retirement

There is also such a thing as academic prostitution. One might apply this label to some television or radio programmes on scientific or historical subjects, but I was invited to do worse by Robert Maxwell when I was at Oxford and he was - among other things - a publisher. He invited me to a *tête-à-tête* lunch at Headington Hall, after which he showed me a lavishly bound and printed book from Germany, of which he wanted to publish an English edition, hopefully with a preface by me. It was of coffee-table format, and consisted of a little text and a lot of coloured photographs, in appalling surgical detail, of the mutilated victims of sexual crimes. Evidently there was a market in Germany for this kind of pornography. I excused myself on the ground that it had no scientific value, and that in any case it was not a subject I knew anything about. He ended the meeting with what I am told was his usual abruptness. I am glad to say that I cannot think of any British criminologist who would have associated himself or herself with such a book. So far as I know it was never published. The nearest thing to it which I have seen in England was the series of slides acquired by the psychiatrist David Stafford-Clark (a showman who wore tartan trews without any ethnic excuse). He used these slides to illustrate a public lecture which an Oxford society invited him to give on 'sexual psychopaths'. Most of the slides were of genital mutilations, in colour. I recall the occasion all the more vividly because I had brought the blind Rupert Cross with me to the lecture, and he demanded that I describe each slide to him.

15. THE AWKWARDNESS OF INNOCENCE

"It is better that some innocent men remain in jail than the integrity of the English judicial system be impugned ..."
(Lord Denning)

Not long before my retirement I tried to entice law reformers into a new field. Criminologists had widened their subjects of study to include the agents of law enforcement and victims of crime. A neglected subject was innocence.

Innocence was not a possibility that troubled republican Romans, but its awkwardness disturbed later Roman lawyers. It is better, said Trajan in the Digest, to let a guilty man go free than punish an innocent one. Trajan probably didn't have in mind a precise one-to-one ratio; but later lawyers who thought they were being liberal proposed higher ratios, ranging from one innocent man in ten to one in twenty, as if the probability could be estimated. More practical was the demand for proof 'beyond reasonable doubt', which makes only a vague stipulation about probability. Nowadays it seems to be acceptable to tell juries that they must be 'sure' or even 'certain'.

Not all judges are troubled by the occasional example of innocence: witness the quotation from Lord Denning at the head of this chapter. One interesting result of the main trend, however, has been that the low probability of innocence which once protected malefactors from death now protects their descendants from probation. Another is that while a low probability is an absolute protection there are situations in which the absence of any evidence of guilt offers no protection at all - for example when a family suffers from the incarceration of a paterfamilias. Some sentencers sometimes take this into account, but that is the exception. A crude excuse for not doing so is that penalising the family is the

170

defendant's fault, not the law's: he should have foreseen it and acted accordingly. A more sophisticated excuse is that the punishment of innocent families is not intentional: it may be avoidable, but the need for something else overrides innocence. That something else is sometimes said to be 'consistency', sometimes - to use the language of the Criminal Justice Act 1992 - 'commensurateness'. A 'commensurate' penalty is what is *deserved* by the offender for his offence.

'Consistency' can of course be justified by a utilitarian argument. Penalties are more effective if not varied. It is utilitarianism, too, which is usually accused of tolerating the penalising of the innocent when this would increase the utility of the penalty. In the best-known scenario by an American author:

"Suppose that in a particular town with a mixed population a man from one racial group rapes a woman from the other group. Because of existing racial tensions the crime is likely to produce racial violence, with many people being injured, unless the guilty man is apprehended quickly. Suppose further that the sheriff of the town can prevent the violence by framing an innocent man who was near the scene of the crime, and who will be accepted by the community as the guilty person. Surely, it is argued, the best consequences will be produced [thus]."

Retributivists use such scenarios as a *reductio ad absurdum*. If that is what a utilitarian penal philosophy means, it is intolerable. As a utilitarian I used to be bothered about this. But is it in fact entailed by a utilitarian philosophy? If a utilitarian finds the scenario morally objectionable is he conceding that the notion of desert must play a part in a penal system?

Herbert Hart suggested a non-retributive reason why a utilitarian ought to ban the conscious penalising of the innocent:

'fairness' rather than 'desert'. But is there a difference between 'unfair' and what the retributivist would call 'undeserved'? I think there is. Imagine two penal systems with only a single difference: one allows the penalising of the innocent when this seems a good idea, the other doesn't. Imagine a person who is offered a choice between being subject to one or the other, but isn't told whether he is likely to be an offender or an innocent (what John Rawls called 'the veil of ignorance'). It is rational for him to choose the one which bans the penalising of the innocent. He need not appeal to 'desert'.

Yet 'fairness' seems to require more protection for the innocent than they get, at least in England. The 'presumption of innocence' is a valuable protection, but its scope is often exaggerated. Although often appealed to in wider contexts (such as the refusal of bail) its legal status is in fact no more than that of a procedural rule for the trial of guilt, which lays the burden of proof upon the prosecution.

If the presumption were a conscientiously held principle of law enforcement it would condemn the public naming of suspects before they have been convicted. Naming is occasionally of practical use, for example when a suspect has made himself hard to find, or is believed to be a danger to others. When that is not the case naming stigmatises a person who may be acquitted. It will not do to argue that an acquittal will remove the stigma. An acquittal merely declares that a conviction would be unsafe, not mistaken, and even people who do not appreciate this are apt to view acquittals with suspicion.

There are countries - most of them in northern Europe - where the identification of suspects before conviction is prohibited, either by law or by convention: but this is rare in common-law countries The New Zealand legislature were persuaded in 1975 to pass an Act which prohibited the naming of suspects until they were convicted, unless a judge had authorised it. The Act worked, but after only a year the news media persuaded a new government to repeal that part of it. In that same year, however, when the British parliament was debating a clause of a Bill which prohibited the public naming of victims of rape, a backbencher moved a successful amendment which extended the protection to men accused of 'rape offences', except in cases in which a court had decided otherwise (I know of only one case in which it did, when a man tried for burglary and rape was jailed for the burglary but acquitted of rape, and didn't want to be regarded as a rapist in prison). This enlightened provision lasted for 12 years, and worked. Research showed that reporting of rape trials by the media had actually increased. Procedural awkwardnesses were rare and trivial. A Basildon man and his wife were both charged with rape. He was convicted, but his wife was acquitted and found guilty only of indecent assault. The news media could not identify him because to do would have identified his wife, contrary to the 1976 Act. As he was sentenced to four years' imprisonment he did not benefit much; but the case was made much of by the media.

In the nineteen eighties I campaigned to extend the protection to other offences, and got many private expressions of agreement - for example from Barbara Wootton and Lord Hunt - but no public support. The All Party Penal Affairs Group dismissed the idea without discussing it with me - or indeed with themselves, since it was disposed of in little more than ten minutes. Finally in 1988 a Government Bill included a clause which improved the law on the identification of victims in rape trials, but allowed defendants to be identified. Opponents of the clause pointed out that identifying the defendant often identified the victim. In such cases identifying an acquitted defendant would stigmatise her as a false accuser, which would be worse than being named as a genuine victim. And since acquittals can be misguided the stigma might be totally unjustified.

What seems to have persuaded most MPs however was an insistence on treating all offences alike, and the protection of acquitted defendants was abolished. It was the end of a promising development.

Now the Home Affairs Committee of the Commons has decided that there is a justification for giving this special protection to defendants in sexual cases.

The passage of the Sexual Offences Bill (summer of 2003) gave Parliament an opportunity to put the clock forward again. In the Lords a former Lord Chief Justice moved a deceptively simple amendment which would grant the defendant in serious sexual cases 'the same right to anonymity as is enjoyed by the complainant'. Doubts were voiced, and the amendment was carried by only 109 to 105 votes. The Home Secretary is said to be opposed; but as the Bill will not be dealt with by the Commons until very late in the session it is possible that the amendment will survive unaltered.

16. BLUE REMEMBERED HILLS

"Before me on either side were high hills, which, by hindering the eye from ranging, forced the mind to find entertainment for itself"

(Samuel Johnston)

Although I have more use for hills than Dr Johnson, a mountaineer as mediocre as I was has of course no right to inflict his reminiscences on anyone else: hence this separate and optional chapter. Yet if I get pleasure from reading other people's recollections of climbing some readers may get the same pleasure from mine.

It was my school-friend Bill Calder who introduced me to hill-walking when I stayed with him in Morayshire. The Cairngorms were only a short drive away, and I still recall our ascent of Braeriach, one of the four-thousand-foot peaks in the Cairngorms. I was a slightly overweight adolescent whose only exercise had been boxing, golf and tennis. The long hot climb from Loch Einich made me gasp for breath, and my leg muscles beg for mercy. The reward was a spectacular view, and I was hooked. After that I persuaded my family that Speyside had more to offer than the seaside, and we walked all over the Cairngorms. We preferred Speyside to Deeside, and I used to climb Ben Avon, Beinn a Bhuird and so on by 30-mile walks from Nethybridge instead of the shorter eastern approaches. Derry, our spaniel, made nothing of these walks, and never seemed even footsore. A minor ambition which I managed to achieve just before the war was 'the four tops' - Cairngorm, Ben Macdhui, Cairntoul and Braeriach, starting from Loch Morlich, where there were no lifts in those days. After the war I helped to carry the parts of Jean's Memorial Hut up to Coire Cas. In winter one could ski over to the Shelter Stone for the night, although I always felt claustrophobic under that titanic lid, and preferred the more open but less snug cave nearby. Nowadays Cairngorm, with its road and ski-lift, is 'fair polluted' with people, as Sergeant Calderwood would have said.

At first I was a Munro-hunter. A century ago a Highland landowner decided to list and climb all the Scottish peaks over 3,000 feet in height, no matter how featureless and dreary, and the name 'Munro' has immortalised his obsession. Obsession is not quite the *mot juste*, but we have no word for the state of mind of people who set themselves a target in order to be able to boast of achieving it (*stochazophilia*, a passion for unnecessary objectives, perhaps?). I prefer to talk of 'Munro hunting', to distinguish it from mountaineering. Some Munro-hunters have even climbed the whole lot in a continuous expedition, followed on the road by fed-up wives in caravans, carrying spare boots. Andrew Dempster's book on Munro-bagging lists them all, but not the broken marriages. What it does chronicle, with naive seriousness, is the recurrent controversy over the very definition of a Munro. Scottish hills being mostly ridges with several bumps, which of the bumps count as 'tops'? Nowadays there is even a list of 'Corbetts', hills between 2,500 and 3,000 feet, which provides a target for those who think they have done all the Munros. Nobody seems to know who Corbett was.

Another pathological trait is an insistence on reaching summits, which are seldom interesting. Most hills - especially in Britain - are just dull humps. Some have interesting cliffs, gullies or aretes. But all these features run out before the summit; and the only spectacular summits are in Skye, Arran and Rhum. What is it that makes some people want to reach the top? As with crime, it is silly to look for a single answer. But sillier still to say, as Mallory did, 'because it's there'. Yet this is the most often quoted explanation, as if it concealed some profundity. Talk of 'conquering' a mountain, as in Smythe's *Kamet Conquered*, is like the talk of big-game hunters: ego-building. Some simple souls just want a good view. Some need an objective to give point to an agreeable walk: Munro-hunting is a pathological intensification of this. Some rock-climbers enjoy the gymnastic problems, but 'tigers' who force new routes up rock and ice are proving that they belong to an elite. Mere curiosity is sometimes the motive. Will that arete, gully or crack 'go'? My own particular enjoyment is a route which traverses the face of a mountain or gorge, with a view both above and below.

Fortunately the war put a stop to my Munro-hunting, and dragged me over so many pointless tops that I lost the taste for it. It is in any case a fussy and blinkered pursuit. Fussy because Munro-hunters wonder whether they have to traverse all the protuberances on a ridge, in case more than one is a Munro. Blinkered because so many of the more interesting hills are slightly below 3,000 feet. The Sleeping Warrior Ridge on Arran offers more exciting scrambling than any Munros outside Skye. The mini-Cuillin on Rhum is another first-class ridge-walk, at least as enjoyable as the slightly more elevated Aonach Eagach in Glencoe. The Cobbler above Loch Long requires a unique head-first wriggle through the eye of its needle. Sutherland's most interesting peak is not one of its scattered Munros, but tiny Stac Polly, with its clusters of basalt columns.

The war put a temporary end to hill-walking for enjoyment. The Lovat Scouts' training in rock-climbing, in Snowdonia, was exciting, and Wigram (of the 1933 Everest expedition) was determined to make all the junior officers 'leaders'. He chased me up routes which scared me stiff, and once, when I found myself spread-eagled between two niches, unable to move hand or foot, I had to hang on for nearly half an hour while he untied himself and eventually dropped a rope from above. He was killed on the same cliff after the war. Wigram tried to cure one poor Glaswegian in my troop whose fear of heights made him nervous even of paths on steep slopes. He devoted a whole day to shepherding Taylor along the Crib Goch ridge, but when they came back at dusk the only noticeable difference was that Taylor's phobia had communicated itself to Wigram, who was picking his way with nervous care.

Being wise after the event I think that our training paid too much attention to climbs of technical difficulty and not enough to coping with really heavy loads and tricky *descents*. Whatever the standard of a route it is always more difficult and dangerous to climb down it - unless one is allowed to abseil, which could leave one fatally exposed to enemy fire. Peace-time rock-climbers count on finding an easier way down. Hardly any televised rock-climbs show a high-grade route being descended without abseiling. The least exciting but most valuable part of our training was in traversing steep ground in full kit without using our hands, which made even the ghillies more sure-footed.

A romantic feature of our winter training in the Canadian Rockies was that the maps of that region had large blank patches, so that one did not know what to expect beyond the next ridge. All our time was spent in learning to ski and stay alive in the winter cold. On one day off, however, I persuaded Major Gibson, who had climbed Mount McKinley, to include me in a one-day attempt on Mount Unwin. Sadly I was so new to glacier skiing, and to crampons, that I slowed the party down, and we barely reached the top before the light began to fail. We were disconcerted to find a box on the summit holding a note signed 'Edmonton Boy Scouts'. Gibson said that couldn't have been a winter ascent, but he was very irritable, and my tardiness on the way down as the light dimmed (the more dangerous part of the little expedition) exasperated him.

We made some interesting discoveries for ourselves. If a rifle is kept overnight in an inhabited tent human vapour will condense inside the barrel, which will then burst when fired, with danger to the firer (but plugging the barrel at night can have the same effect if one forgets to unplug it). A Mills grenade or a small mortar bomb can explode very close in *soft* snow without even wounding. Urinating in sub-zero winds can lead to frost-bite in seconds. Snow-blindness can strike even on dull days at high altitudes. Cooking in snow-holes can cause carbon-monoxide poisoning (which I experienced myself). And so on. No doubt all this and more is now text-book knowledge, but it wasn't then.

After the war it was a year or two before I could enjoy climbing again. I skied a little, but Scottish snow is unreliable at best and alternates between ice and slush, so that decent holidays abroad had to be planned and companions organised. My unlucky right leg got broken in Austria, and later a meniscus had to be removed from that knee, so that it rattles. But climbing was the greater pleasure. Even in Edinburgh one could do a quick illicit rock-scramble up the Crags on Arthur's Seat if one kept one's eye open for park-keepers. It was sheer curiosity which helped me to discover the Cat Nick on the Radical Road. The Pentland Hills and the Lammermuirs are dull: what Johnson called 'an expanse of sullen vegetation', but Glencoe was only a few hours' drive away. A Scottish Mountaineering Club bus would dump us at Lagangarbh on a Friday evening, so that we could be away up the Aonach Eagach ridge in time for a moonlight traverse to Clachaig. Clachaig Gully was above my standard, and I agreed with W.H. Murray that it had 'all the monstrous charm of an elephant's backside'. Murray's books were inspiring, and I went to one Scottish Mountaineering Club dinner simply to hear his after-dinner speech. What put me off those dinners was the narcissistic song about 'my great hobnailers'. I wonder what they sing about now that boots have rubber soles.

There are dozens of good books about mountains, and a lot of mediocre poetry. I can't think of a first-class poet who has made them the subject of a first-class poem, and I'm not forgetting Wordsworth. Housman's 'blue remembered hills' were an optical illusion, the atmospheric effect of distance. It's said that he didn't even visit Shropshire until he had published *A Shropshire Lad*. Poetasters like Winthrop Young were inspired by male companionship, by the exhilaration of gymnastic exercise, by machismo, by trepidation, by achievement - all things that non-poets can enjoy without being told how.

What I haven't found in the literature either is an appreciation of the occasional *creepiness* of big hills. Historians record that in earlier centuries travellers in the Alps would often feel obliged to shield their eyes from the terrifying view; but that is not quite the same feeling. Once, on a dark day in the Cairngorms, it made me run out of a corrie, not stopping until I realised that my spaniel Derry was merely puzzled by the exertion. On the other hand when I spent one or two nights in a tent by the site of the Glencoe Massacre no visitation disturbed my dreams. As for the Brocken Spectre, it is impressive rather than unearthly, being a fairly common spectacle in the Cuillin. It is worth noting that it is only one's own huge shadow that has a halo, and never one's companions'.

Spirituality and superstition are all very well. Competitiveness is not. Alan Clark's *Diaries* occasionally refer to his climbs, but only to record that he beat someone to the top. A hill shouldn't be treated as a proving-ground. Nor as a place for arm-wrestling with death. That was what repelled me about some of the rock-climbers I used to meet in Glencoe or the Cuillin. They boasted of 'coming off' and being saved by a firm belay or a snow-filled gully. Fatalities were news but not tragedies. There were of course risks that had to be taken, not sought. On one of our easy routes on Tarneilar a boulder rolled over on Jock Rushforth (now an ex-Commando g.p.

with a Normandy wound), leaving him with a continuous tartan bruise from arm to thigh. Some stone-falls are the droppings of clumsy climbers above. The compass, too, is of no use in the Cuillin because of the rock's iron content, so that in mist one can mistakenly descend a suicidal ridge or gully. Later, when I got to know the Dolomites, I came to the conclusion that the rock, the weather and the people made the tiny Cuillin more hazardous.

I am sorry that I never made the complete traverse of the ridge, from Garsbheinn to Sgur nan Ghillean; but I am in good company. The competitive John Buchan planned to be the first to do it, but when he found that 'others were before me' decided that this let him off. Nowadays the traverse is not regarded as a feat unless one includes the Red Cuillin (i.e. Clach Glas and Blaven), which entails the wearisome crossing of Glen Sligachan. I believe that the record is just under 12 hours from first to final top.

A tiny version of the Cuillin is the ridge on Rhum, with the same mixture of gabbro and loose basalt. In the days when the island was privately owned by an absentee landlord, and repelled landers, I managed to get permission from the family's solicitors to spend a few days there, provided that I made no demands on its 16 inhabitants for food or shelter. Jock Rushforth and I took a tent and several dozen hard-boiled eggs, which remained edible, though curiously discoloured, for the whole of our stay. The traverse of the ridge ends at the little bay where Sir George Bulloch rests in a mini-Theseum of white marble. He was the last purchaser of the island before the National Trust, and like my romantic adjutant insisted that the builders of his castle wear kilts. Their views are not on record.

On our last night the gale was so strong and wet that the head stalker gave us shelter - not of our asking - and we spent an evening listening to his stories. He was fierce about the poachers who came by boat from Mallaig to take his deer, and he had been known to put a rifle bullet through their boat below its waterline. Sitting silent in the shadowy corner of his living-room was a beautiful Neapolitan girl whom his soldier son had married and dumped in this barely inhabited island. She must have felt like Julia on Pantellaria.

My return to Oxford in my forties meant the renewal of my friendship with Bill Calder, whom I hadn't seen since the war. He was now the tutor in German at Queens', and I managed to persuade him and several other friends to explore the Dolomites with me, starting at Cortina. In those days an overnight train journey in couchettes was involved, and I thought I had managed to get us all into a six-couchette compartment. The next compartment had been booked for nuns; but the French train service had put our psychiatrist, Henry Rollin, in with five nuns, and in his place with us was an embarrassed school-girl. When the senior nun came down the train one of the junior nuns complained that a man had been put in their compartment. The senior nun snapped 'And why not?' In theory we were impressed, but in practice sympathised with the junior nuns, and in spite of obstruction from the train attendant quietly swapped a school-girl for a psychiatrist.

At Cortina the Astaldi route up Tofana was our first experience of a fairly exposed *via ferrata* (a rock route with safety cables at awkward places), and also our first experience of the pleasures to be found in *rifugi*, most of which offered satisfying if expensive food and drink halfway up the mountain. This was the first of a series of summer expeditions which I organised for more than 20 years, involving Henry Rollin, Henry Pelling, Jenifer Hart, Alan Ryan, Carol Graham-Harrison, David Edwards, Peter Heath, David Widdicombe and later, as these friends dropped out for one reason or another, my sister, her husband and my nephew Michael Potter. (My wife's physical condition ruled out climbing; but she never tried to discourage me).

The Dolomites are known for their perpendicular pinnacles and faces, of a high degree of difficulty, but are also ideal for the middle-aged who want a little safe excitement. The multi-coloured peaks make spectacular scenery, especially in the violet flashes of thunderstorms, but nearly all can be climbed or circumvented by routes that would rank as 'easy' or 'moderate' in Scotland, or with the help of a *via ferrata*. As for snow and ice I had learned in the Rockies to dislike them, and was glad to find that they could be avoided on almost every Dolomite ascent. The rock is so sound that in the summer rockfalls are rare, although I once saw a lump the size of a bus fall off the flank of Fradusta, in the San Martino group. Most of the major peaks are only about 10,000 feet in height, and ski-lifts reduce most climbs to 5,000 feet or less.

Once or twice, in the days when guides charged reasonable fees, I took one for a harder rock-climb than I could lead. Not all guides were faultless. One bounced a small piece of rock off me when we were doing a short, cheap, climb on Piz Tchir. In Cortina I found Celso de Gasper, by then over 60, who agreed to take me up the Torre Grande by the *via normale* for a modest sum. Halfway up he flattered me about my style, and offered a variation by way of a more difficult route. I agreed without dreaming that it would add 50 per cent to his fee. His chicanery was easy to forgive, however, because of his memories, which stretched back to the First World War, when the Austrian troops were just above Cortina on the Falzarego Pass. His cousin had been on the Austrian side, and told him how they had tunnelled into a pinnacle on the side of the Tofana range to set up a gunner's observation post. After some days the men in the post heard the sound of metal striking rock below them, and realised that they were being mined. When the gunnery subaltern reported this he was told to stay put until the sound of mining stopped - a sign that the time had come for the tunnel to be packed with explosives. At this stage the officer and his men were withdrawn, but replaced by another half-dozen who were not told what their predecessors had heard. Two nights later the Italians blew them all to scree.

Strictly speaking, the jagged Latemar, south of the well-known Rosengarten, is not a Dolomite ridge, being composed of some much more brittle rock. This has shattered, however, in fascinating ways, and the traverse is worth the trouble of reaching it. Conversely the Brenta, though well to the south-west of the main Dolomites, is made of the same colourful limestone, with towers and ridges of the same sharpness. Its weather, unfortunately, is worse. In most Dolomite valleys one can escape persistent rain or cloud by moving to a valley down wind; but not in the Brenta. Its higher precipitation means that some of the passes have *vedrettas*, small glaciers without crevasses, and some of the tops call for ice-axes.

It was a few years before I discovered the Brenta. Its foul summer weather is offset by the attraction of the high-level *via ferrata* which traverses a series of spectacular faces and towers. The northernmost section, just east of Campo Carlomagno, was the creation of a priest with both vision and spare time. It takes vision of a special sort to see how a series of ledges and gullies on a perpendicular face can be economically linked by safety-cables and ladders so that even someone of retiring age, as I was, can feel secure, if exhausted (I had taken a week-end off on the way to a symposium in Sicily, and was far from fit). Sicily provided an opportunity for a quick bus-ride up Etna, but tourists were forbidden to approach the crater because nine had been killed by a mini-eruption the week before. I had had a better view of Etna in the small plane from Milan. From my seat just behind the cockpit it was visible straight ahead. The pilot was gossiping with a girl, until she pointed out how close we were getting to the mountain.

The result was a sharp swerve.

Most of the friends who came on my Dolomite holidays enjoyed them enough to come again. Our only accident in 20 years was Henry Rollin's sprained ankle, and nobody quarrelled. The only incident which grated was one don's anti-clerical jeers at a priest who was celebrating a harmless mass with some children in front of the cross on Piz Boe. The priest of course paid no attention, and it was the rest of us who were embarrassed. The most popular member of the group was Bill Calder, with his unvarying good humour and wit. By now, in middle age, he looked strikingly like Jeffrey Archer, but kindlier. It was when climbing with him that I saw how much alcohol now meant to him. He was the only man I knew who needed a brandy at breakfast, scandalising the hotel staff. After breakfast he would load his rucksack with cans of beer, several of which, to do him justice, he generously gave away during a long day. But an increasing intake of alcohol eventually put an end to his climbing, and finally to his life. He had a stroke in his sixties, and spent more than ten years in a nursing-home. Humanely the nurses turned a blind eye to his little expeditions 'to buy a newspaper', from which he would return refreshed. Unknown to me he died at the age of 82.

Another popular member was Jenifer Hart, with her violent but amusing views on history, literature, morality, politics and political correctness. Several of my friends and acquaintances have written autobiographies, but the one I most enjoyed was hers - *Ask me No More*. The quotation is from Housman, and goes on *for fear I should reply*. Certainly there must have been people who feared what she might have replied if asked for more. I myself was let off lightly as one of the 'civilised' members of my college. Gossip apart, however, the merit of the book is its frank account of her ambitions, affections and disasters, told with both humanity and a modesty which is unusual in autobiographies.

Turn the Dolomites upside down and you have the Grand Canyon, which I managed to visit twice in the course of academic expeditions. The two-day walk from the south to north rims was an unforgettable experience. Some people manage the hot 5,000-foot descent and 6,000-foot ascent in a single day; but most spend a night in the 'ranch' by the Colorado River. In my sixties that was my choice. That year the bunkhouse was being rebuilt, however, and all one could reserve was a six-by-three-foot space for one's sleeping-bag. No reservation meant no overnight stay in this strictly regulated spot. The next plots to mine had been allotted to a policewoman from Denver and her teenage son, who had persuaded her to buy her first pair of walking boots for the expedition. I have never, in all my time in the army, seen feet as bloody as that poor woman's. I left her in the charge of a doctor and his wife. The climb up to the north rim was made memorable by a sudden thunderstorm, its darkness periodically lit up by violet lightning strikes against the cliff beside the path. Later that week I found an old, little-used miners' path, and spent an unreserved night beside a spring, disturbed by wild burros and a raccoon which rummaged in my rucksack. Almost as exciting next morning was meeting a rattlesnake on my path, one of the Grand Canyon species with drab colours and a small rattle. There was no confrontation: he was just as disinclined for one as I was.

A sabbatical term at Berkeley allowed me two week-ends of climbing in the Sierras. Yosemite valley was as crowded as a Butlin camp in July, but after twenty minutes' uphill walking there were few people to be seen. The really hard rock-climbing is on El Capitan, the 3,000-foot cliff which looms over the main valley. I went for Half-Dome, an equally daunting sight, but with an easy path up its southern flank. The last few hundred feet require one to cross a steep slope of bare granite above an enormous drop, but steps have been cut in it. It was a gusty day, but an adult was in no danger. What horrified me was the sight of a boy of about six following his father down the slope with nothing to secure him against a two thousand-foot fall. I found it difficult to convince his father that his son's life was at risk. I have noticed the same incomprehensible insouciance in Italian parents in the Dolomites, yet the Italian newspapers never report fatalities of this kind. Perhaps they are too common?

On another long week-end I visited the 9,000-foot Tioga Pass, above Yosemite. Here was a Cairngorm-like plateau topped by mounds of granite, hundreds of feet high and rounded into gigantic pillows, with slopes that look easy until you realise, halfway up, how holdless they are. Easier was the scramble up a 12,000-foot peak, lightly dusted with July snow, that looked down 6,000 feet to the baking Mono Desert. Rushing up from sea-level at Berkeley to sleep at the Pass and climb next day made me realise what a severe migraine is like.

At Cape Town, Table Mountain enlivened some rather wet weeks of seminar-giving. The campus is beautifully sited on the lower slopes, and after a morning class I could take General Smuts' steep walk up Skeleton Gorge to the plateau. I was told that the plateau was inhabited by 'bergies' - men who lived rough up there in the mild climate, and were not above robbery; but the only one I met conversed harmlessly. The face of the Devil's Peak was more challenging, rather like Buchaille Etive Mhor with added vegetation, and I spent an enjoyable afternoon trying to make a gully 'go'. It got steeper and steeper, and the boulders looser, so that eventually I had to traverse out of it onto the face, coming nose-to-nose with a startled klipspringer, the Cape equivalent of a chamois. On the lower slopes of another hill, further inland, the thorn-bush was so dense that we had to crawl along tunnels made in it by some wild animal. The curse of the bush where deer abound is a tick which carries a particularly nasty fever, so that we had been warned to search each other's clothing after passing through bush, and spent a lot of time doing so. Later I learned that there is the same danger in the scrub of the Tyrol, but that this information is not disclosed to tourists.

Until I was in my seventies I didn't know that the Picos d'Europa existed in northern Spain, quite separate from the Pyrenees, north of the pilgrim route to Compostela. My military Italian had equipped me for solitary expeditions in the Dolomites, but I had no confidence in my phrase-book Spanish, so decided to join a commercial holiday group. Being by now well into my seventies I was required to present a medical certificate, but was made welcome by the rather younger members. The group had a professional leader, who spoke fluent Spanish with a Peruvian accent - and sympathised politically with the murderous guerrillas of the Shining Path. Unfortunately he was a last-minute substitute for a leader who had been familiar with the terrain, and all he had were some very rough notes. As a result he involved us in several abortive sallies, including a difficult descent of the wrong valley. On another day he was about to lead us across a dangerously steep snow-slope without ropes or ice-axes, and had to be dissuaded. As it was August I had expected heat but not the humidity. Rain and low cloud from the Bay of Biscay was an almost daily nuisance. On one of the fine days, having too small a water-bottle, I experienced real dehydration, something I had not encountered, even when heavily laden, in the Appennines or Arizona. Exhaustion and a racing pulse were alarming, but disappeared as soon as we found a spring. Some of the Picos is just a high moor, with the tedious repetitiveness of the Monadliaths, but an attractive feature is a seven-mile path halfway up the side of a 3,000-foot gorge, where the walker is hovered over by two species of vulture, both optimistic in the tourist season.

My last climbing holiday, at the end of my seventies, was spent in the Dolomites with my nephew Michael Potter, and ended with the splendid walk from Bolzano to Merano, along a forested plateau. I had been experiencing some breathlessness on uphill stretches in the mountains, and back in Cambridge found myself suddenly coming to unplanned halts. These proved to be the precursors of a mild heart attack, and I was warned not to try any more high walking. Once again it was sheer luck that had saved me, by postponing the attack until my return from the Dolomites. It frightened me off cigars as well as climbing. In the intensive care unit I did find a young hospital doctor who said that one cigar a day would probably do no harm, but he was transferred next day to the renal unit, which weakened his credibility. I had had practice in overcoming an addiction to nicotine, having given up my wartime smoking for a quarter of a century, but had taken up cigars in the sixties to relieve the tensions of university squabbling.

My next piece of luck was also medical, but had a tragic aspect. The urologist who kept an eye on my prostate cancer by means of the usual blood-tests and biopsies advised me that my tumour was normal for my age, and did not call for drastic treatment. He was a nice man, and I was saddened by his sudden death from a heart attack. My new consultant took quite a different view, and prescribed immediate radiotherapy, which another consultant said had saved my life, or more precisely made it likelier that I would die of something else. Spared again by Providence without deserving it, as Nurse Cook would have said. One can be superstitious about luck, and I am not looking forward to my 86th birthday because that was the age at which my father died - an example of superstition supported by genetics. Yet for all I know there may be more luck to come. The sorrow for an atheist is that he has nobody to be grateful to.

INDEX

Mannheim, Herman 96, 119,
121
Manuel, Peter (serial rapist and
murderer) 79-80
Margaret, Princess 45
Mark, Commissioner Robert 89,
95-6
Marsh, Catherine 151
Martial 11
Martin, John 165
Marx and Marxism 122, 159
Mason, James 24, 25
Maudsley Hospital 97, 168
Mauretania S.S. 47
Maxwell, James Clerk 12
Maxwell, Robert 168
McAlpine, Ida 100
McCabe, Sarah 104-5, 106, 149
McGrath, Pat 104
McLintock, Derick 97, 125
Melville, Leslie 44, 49, 57, 60
Mental Health Act (1959) 104
mental hospitals 94, 95
mental illness 78, 104-6, 115,
130, 149
Merano 189
Merton, Robert 146
Middle East 36, 47
Mill, John Stuart 145
Milton 28, 55
Ministry of Health 63
M'Naghten 105
Monks of St Giles 71, 81
Morris, Pauline 93
Morris, Terence 93, 96

Morrison, Donald 19, 22, 28
mortars 38-9, 52, 56, 179
Munro-hunting 176-7
murder 18, 82-3, 96, 97, 110,
148, 154
capital punishment 77-82,
123, 143
Murdoch, Iris 91
Murray, WH 179

naming of parts 31, 42
naming of suspects 172-3
Naples 49, 50
National Association of
Probation Officers (NAPO)
136-7, 147
National Health Service 63, 64
National Library of Scotland
109
National Trust 181
nepotism 166
New Criminologists 122, 144-5
Newhaven Chess Club 135
Newnham College 116-17
Newsam, Frank 77, 81
Nicol, Andrew 117
Noble (army officer) 33, 44
Norris, Sidney 113
North Uist 42
Norway 41, 43, 49, 70
Norwood East 98
Nuffield College 86-92, 93-111,
116, 142

Oakland 107